Professional Ethics in Context

Other books by Eric Mount, Jr.

Conscience and Responsibility
The Feminine Factor

Professional Ethics in Context

Institutions, Images, and Empathy

Eric Mount, Jr.

Westminster/John Knox Press
Louisville, Kentucky

Scripture quotations from the Revised Standard Version of the Bible are copyrighted 1946, 1952, © 1971, 1973 by the Division of Christian Education of the National Council of the Churches of Christ in the U.S.A. and are used by permission.

The quotation by Michael Ignatieff found at the opening of chapter 4 is taken from "Modern Dying," *The New Republic* (December 26, 1988), p. 32. Copyright 1989, United Feature Syndicate, Inc.

The quotation by George Kennan on p. 97 is taken from "George Kennan Calls on U.S. to View Soviet More Soberly," *The New York Times* (November 18, 1981). Copyright © 1981 by The New York Times Company. Reprinted by permission.

Book design by Gene Harris

First edition

Published by Westminster/John Knox Press
Louisville, Kentucky

PRINTED IN THE UNITED STATES OF AMERICA

9   8   7   6   5   4   3   2   1

Library of Congress Cataloging-in-Publication Data

Mount, Eric.
  Professional ethics in context : institutions, images, and empathy / Eric Mount, Jr. — 1st ed.
        p.   cm.
  Includes bibliographical references.
  ISBN 0-664-25143-9

  1. Professional ethics.   I. Title.
BJ1725.M68   1990
174—dc20   90-33574
                                                        CIP

In loving memory
of
Charles Eric Mount
and
Virginia Lander Mount
Devoted Christian servants,
partners, and parents

Contents

Preface

This book has had such a long gestation period that it is hard to know when to start the roll call of those who have helped it come to birth. My projects in summer seminars of the National Endowment for the Humanities with Robert Bellah (1976) and James Childress (1981) stimulated my interest in further exploring individualism as America's myth and the importance of myth, model, and metaphor in a nation's approach to the provision of health care. During my year as a traveling humanities professor for the Kentucky Humanities Council (1979–80), I developed some of the themes of this book in the lectures and programs I gave. A 1983 sabbatical from my teaching at Centre College was supposed to have been the time to get the projected book written, but accepting my friend Rich Morrill's invitation to become vice-president and dean of students meant postponing the leave. The summer demands of the position allowed only the preparation of a first draft during part of the summer of 1985. Writing this version in light of responses to that first draft had to await a 1988–89 sabbatical following completion of my term in the dean's office. In a way I am as indebted to those who kept me from finishing the job sooner (and thereby failing to include some crucial features) as I am to those whose support, cooperation, criticism, and encouragement enabled me to get the book completed at last.

President Morrill and the Centre administration allowed me to accumulate sabbatical credit and thus to take a year's leave at full pay. Vanderbilt University gave me the privileges of a visiting scholar, and Dick Zaner, Bob Crumby, Gene Copello, and Gabriele Wood of the Center for Clinical and Research Ethics made the 1988 fall semester at Vanderbilt an ideal period for launching this endeavor. Don Welch of the Vanderbilt Law School and "Pat" Rettew of the Owen School of Management offered helpful reactions and suggestions as I was getting started. The First Presbyterian Church of Nashville and its senior minister Bill Bryant provided both a comfortable place to live and a stimulating setting to trial-teach the main features of the book.

As for attention to the manuscript itself, numerous long-suffering friends have read and assessed all or parts of these chapters and the earlier draft. My friend Rollin Tarter, chief administrator of a community mental health agency and occasional religion instructor at Centre, leads the list because he "went the second manuscript" and read all of both. Anonymous readers for John Knox Press offered much appreciated encouragement and appropriate criticism. Centre friends and colleagues gave me invaluable reactions—Rich Morrill, now at the University of Richmond, and Milton Scarborough especially to the book's argument and Charles Hazelrigg especially to matters of syntax and style. Vanderbilt's Dick Zaner both enriched my thinking through his writing and our friendship and endorsed the chapters I wrote while I was with him. Gabriel Smilkstein, who teaches at the University of Louisville Medical School, even burdened a European vacation with my manuscript and brought back cogent observations. Walt Sutton of Westminster/John Knox Press patiently offered assistance and encouragement over a period longer than either of us might have preferred. And copy editor Linda Benefield provided both generous reinforcement and skillful remedies.

My family has provided the greatest help of all. As in everything else, Truly, my beloved partner of thirty-one years, constantly helped me keep things in perspective and yet aided and encouraged my work—editing and proofreading, enduring and believing. Lawyer daughter Diane and public health graduate student daughter Laurie have furnished invaluable editorial advice about the latest version and typing assistance on the first draft. Collegiate daughters Marcia and Mary Faith have given fresh and helpful reactions to portions of the project. Son-in-law John Nisbet got me out of many jams as I learned to use a word processor. Both Diane and John, who is also an attorney, gave me considerable insight into the process of legal education, as did Laurie on the preparation of public health professionals. And then there was O'Malley, our faithful family pointer. This family made life good apart from writing books, yet they also made me want to write this book.

My first book, *Conscience and Responsibility*, was the offspring of the research I did for my doctoral dissertation. My second one, *The Feminine Factor*, was triggered to a large degree by my wife's negotiation of the combined roles of wife and mother on the one hand and of graduate student and teacher on the other and by my dreams for the futures of our four daughters. This current book has grown out of twenty-four years of studying ethics with Centre undergraduates, my friendships with professional colleagues from the Centre faculty and elsewhere, my association with groups of business and professional leaders in discussions of moral questions in institutional settings, and my experiences with staff members, students, and structures during three stints in the Centre administration. Perhaps even more than the valued authors and teachers who have shaped my thinking and whose names can be found in the text and notes of the book, my daily companions in the mutual formation of character, in the address of ethical questions, and in the struggle to make responsible decisions have influenced and enriched what is found in these pages. Therefore, my fellow learners and companions in conscientious pilgrimage both in my family and professional life have my deepest gratitude.

In short, more people than I can name deserve credit for this book, but not one of them deserves blame for it. If you are disappointed in what you find here, just believe that it would not have been nearly as good as it is without all the help.

1
Seeing Is Behaving

"If you could just see facts flat on, without that horrible moral squint; with just a little common sense, you could have been a statesman."

Cardinal Wolsey to Sir Thomas More
in *A Man for All Seasons*
by Robert Bolt

The eye is the lamp of the body. So, if your eye is sound, your whole body will be full of light; but if your eye is not sound, your whole body will be full of darkness. If then the light in you is darkness, how great is the darkness!

Matthew 6:22–23

It was a telling moment, one of those times when something you thought you already knew really came home to you. A group of local business executives had gathered to discuss ethical issues in management with some of us academic types. A new plant manager in town and I were trading views about the merits of a wholly unregulated market and the extent to which people are or are not self-made. In what I thought was a master stroke, I quoted British Bishop Charles Gore's description of laissez-faire capitalism: " 'Each for himself and God for us all,' said the elephant as he danced among the chickens."[1] Hank was totally unimpressed with my effort to create sympathy for the underchickens. He retorted, "Let the chickens learn to fly." From Hank's perspective, the chickens were fully capable of getting out from under foot and rising to the top.

As I learned more about Hank and thought more about myself, I realized that it would have been better to begin the first of our group's discussions by asking each participant to tell his or her story, instead of immediately inviting reactions to a case study that presented a moral problem. Learning where each of us was coming from was crucial to our understanding of how we looked at things, and how we saw things accounted more for our differences than the moral principles we might invoke in addressing an ethical issue.[2] Hank and I soon became friendly in our conversations, but we never came to like each other's "looks."

The Root of Moral Conflict: Where We Are Coming From

It turned out that Hank had come from modest beginnings. Growing up on his family's dirt farm, he had worked to help them scratch out a living. He had vied with siblings, he had struggled to get an education in business management, and he had fought to rise to his position of corporate leadership. In Hank's view, anyone who wanted to succeed badly enough could do what he had done; he had little patience with those who failed to better themselves. He saw himself as an embodiment of the American dream—that national myth or morality tale was his story.

On the other side of the table sat a college professor of religion and ethics. I was the son of two well-educated people, the only child and the only grandchild in a minister's family, the debtor to a series of excellent schools, the beneficiary of several scholarships and fellowships, and the reaper of numerous benefits as a faculty member and administrator in a strong academic institution.

Of course, Hank had gained his position with more than a little help from his friends, family, teachers, and co-workers. And I was no stranger to competition in school or in athletics. I had earned a doctorate in three years with a family and a part-time job, not only because of my privileges, but also because of what one of my seminary professors described as the twin requisites for a Ph.D.—an iron will and an iron butt. Despite those similarities, Hank and I perceived the world very differently, and our numerous disagreements were rooted more in our perceptions than in our principles. We worshiped in the same congregation; we both believed in "liberty and justice for all"; we both felt the influence of the American dream; and we were both trying to live our lives with integrity. Yet our outlooks were different. Liberty, justice, and the American dream called up different images in our minds.

There was a moment in the 1988 presidential campaign when similar diversities of outlook emerged in stark opposition. During the debate between the vice-presidential candidates, Senators Bentsen and Quayle were asked to recall an especially formative experience in their personal development. Speaking first, Senator Quayle recounted the advice that his grandmother, Martha Pulliam, had given to him when he was a boy: "You can do anything you want to, if you just set your mind to it and go to work." When his turn came, Senator Bentsen recalled growing up near the Mexican border and seeing the poverty and educational need of the Mexican-Americans. Both men were born to privilege, and both strove to capitalize on what they had received, but one man's philosophy centered on climbing the ladder of success, while the other man concerned himself with the rungs that were missing on the ladders of others. Both focused on the American dream, a powerful expression of our societal values. But they viewed the dream differently; as a result, they saw other things differently.

Jesse Jackson also appealed to a version of the American dream when he said that he was born in a ghetto, but the ghetto was not born in him. In exhorting the young to stay away from drugs and to stop blaming their problems on others and to make something of themselves, he drew on that same American myth or cultural story, but because of where he started out, Jackson was coming from a point of view different from that of Senator Quayle in quoting his grandmother. In a comparable way, Vice President Bush and Governor Dukakis both set their campaigns in the context of the American dream, but they saw and expressed the meaning of that national myth differently.

Leaving aside any further pursuit of the reasons for the different outlooks of recent American political candidates, I return to Hank and me. What gave us our different outlooks? We had diverse family beginnings, and our lives had, of course, unfolded through varying and incalculable combinations of factors. Could more be said to explain our differences?

For one thing, any education does more for you and to you than provide helpful information, and professional education definitely instills a particular slant on things. James R. Elkins, professor of law at West Virginia University and past president of the American Legal Studies Association, illustrates this transformation in his article "Becoming a Lawyer: The Transformation of Self During Legal Education." He observes, "To become a lawyer is to change one's story dramatically." In keeping with our theme of vision, he believes "Law is a theory, a means to see or behold the world. The Latin roots of the word 'theory' are related to the word 'theater,' which can be defined as a place for seeing. Thus, law, or a theory of law, is a place for seeing."[3]

During a health policy seminar on organ transplantation at Vanderbilt University in December of 1988, Jerold R. Mande, Senator Albert Gore's legislative assistant specializing in transplant issues, cited conflicting visions as basic to policy disagreements. Mande spoke of a lawyer's vision, an economist's vision, a transplant surgeon's vision, and an ethicist's vision. People with those conflicting visions start with different ways of sizing up the issues, and those different starting points or vantage points have to be understood if any meetings of the minds are to occur. In that light, business school and theological seminary did different things to Hank and me.

The institutional setting in which people work each day also has a profound effect on their perceptions. Hank and I had been inhabiting the different vocational worlds of corporate life and college life. In those different worlds, different languages are spoken. Reports meant company quarterly earnings statements to him and either committee recommendations or student grades to me. I knew what the bottom line meant, but my conversation was not liberally sprinkled with the term. Different metaphors and images filtered our perceptions of ourselves and others. He thought of himself as a football coach who was always plotting strategy to win the game within the rules or as a fighter who was struggling against hostile forces in the business environment for survival and profitability. Depending on the time of day, I might see myself as a midwife helping students bring to life their potential, a Socratic gadfly raising unsettling questions, a counselor easing someone through a tough time, or an adviser guiding a student's planning of the next term's schedule. The images of the midwife and the gadfly would have probably had little or no appeal for Hank.

Different stories expressed the traditions of Hank's institution and mine. Those stories exalted different heroes, who were revered as examples of different values. I could explore the books and magazines Hank and I read or the friends we valued most, but the point is that different outlooks shaped our perceptions of issues, of people, and of situations. Different institutional surroundings set the limits and opened the possibilities for our daily moral thinking and acting.

What was true for Hank and me holds true for the lion's share of ethical impasses among people. They are real, not imaginary; yet they are rooted in our imaginations, in the way we perceive things, more than in ethical principles or rules. They grow out of (1) our differing educational and vocational environments; (2) the differing metaphors that shape our perceptions of moral issues, and differing images of ourselves, of others, of society, of the natural world, and of whatever god or center of loyalty provides us with our integrity; (3) the differing worldviews or ideologies or myths (or differing understandings of commonly espoused myths or values, like the American dream or "liberty and justice for all") that provide our lives with both setting and standpoint; and (4) our differing life experiences. All these differences put us in different places in which to be the people we are becoming and different vantage points from which to see the moral life.

These contexts are both settings and lenses for vision, both our points of contact for moral development and choice and our points of view for perception and interpretation of moral matters. They locate us and they give us eyes for only some sights and not for others. To fail to place people in the various worlds they inhabit is to miss seeing them as they are. To fail to perceive people's contact lenses or filters of vision as part of the situations of moral interaction is to miss seeing people as they see. For us to address specific moral problems together, it helps greatly to begin by facing differences in "where we are coming from" and "where in the world we are" as moral interpreters, evaluators, decision-makers, and actors. In the following pages, the surroundings and outlooks that condition our ethical thought and action will emerge as the focuses of our attention.

On August 19, 1985, as the violence in South Africa mounted, and after Prime Minister P. W. Botha had made a speech ruling out eventual equal political participation by the black majority, leaders of South Africa's multiracial Christian churches met with Botha. Following the meeting, Archbishop Denis E. Hurley, chairman of the Southern African Catholic Bishops Conference, said, "Our two perceptions of South Africa are so different that we hardly began to communicate at all." Since the two sides approached the situation from different understandings of the nation's history, within different frames of reference, and from mostly separated cultures, it is little wonder they could not communicate.

In more recent meetings between two leaders who had inherited long legacies of antagonism between their respective nations, General Secretary Gorbachev and President Reagan made considerable progress in communication, and the introduction of new metaphors had more than a little to do with it. The evil empire metaphor or image that President Reagan had used early in his presidency gave way to the metaphors of *glasnost* (openness) and *perestroika* (restructuring) introduced by Gorbachev. The new metaphors helped to shape a new outlook on the two countries' relationship, and the two men began to hold a world in common. During a visit to the United States in early December of 1988, the Soviet leader delivered a memorable speech before the United Nations General Assembly in which he offered substantial unilateral troop reductions and spoke of addressing together the problems of a shared world. The rhetoric of Khrushchev about burying the United States was a thing of the past. Soon after the speech, President Reagan held the last press conference of his presidency. He announced that he had sent Mr. Gorbachev a picture of the two of them walking together during the general secretary's previous visit. The inscription read: "We have walked a long way together to clear a path for peace."

President Reagan's adversarial posture had changed. The two men could see each other differently because they looked through new linguistic lenses.

The Root of Moral Action: Seeing Is Behaving

In asserting that "moral behavior is an affair not primarily of choice but of vision,"[4] Stanley Hauerwas is in effect saying that seeing is behaving. When people say that seeing is believing, they mean, "I would have to see it to believe it." Our claim is a different one: To see is to behave. When it comes to sizing up a situation ethically, the way we see it profoundly affects the response we consider right. We need to see the situation before we are prompted to do something about it.

Seeing includes imagining alternative futures, not just reviewing current conditions. People differ over the new possibilities they can foresee emerging from a bad situation. We respond not only to what we see before us; we also behave in light of what we anticipate. Hopeful people often bring their dreams to fruition because they act in light of the prospects they envision.

Seeing is behaving also carries another layer of meaning. Seeing is an act. It is not merely the passive registry of impressions. As Cardinal Wolsey put it in the quotation at the head of the chapter, we look with some kind of "moral squint." We focus. We scan. We search. We scrutinize. We stare. We give dirty looks. When we look into things, we may take close looks, quick looks, good looks, hard looks, long looks, or honest looks. We can look with favor or disfavor. We look around; we look askance; and we overlook things. We look down on people, up to people, and out for people. We speculate (literally, "spy out"). We inspect, respect, and expect (originally "exspect"). With some linguistic license, we can say that we introspect, retrospect, circumspect, and prospect (for more than gold). More often than not, we see what we want to see. Sometimes, when our defenses are down, we get hit between the eyes with something we had no desire to see, but usually we are experts at blocking out or filtering out unsettling sights. As sixteenth-century poet John Heywood asks, "Who is so deafe, or so blynde as is hee/ That willfully will nother hear nor see?"

An outlook depends on who is on the lookout. Our morality is not just a matter of what we decide and what we do; it is based on who we are as viewers and interpreters of what is going on. Our personal identities and powers of discernment depend on "where we are coming from" with our worldviews and linguistic filters of experience, and where we are situated in relationships and institutions. The seer is an evaluator as she sees, not just after she has sized up the situation.[5]

By saying that seeing is willful, we tell the truth, but not the whole truth. Refusal to see is the worst kind of blindness, but it is the worst because of the culpability of the cause, not the severity of the effect. Blindness is not only an intention; it can be an affliction. In Alice Walker's *The Color Purple*, two black women engage in a powerful conversation about the way they envision God. Because of all she has suffered and the futility of her letters to God, Celie sees no reason to keep on believing. Shug becomes her guide to a new way of seeing God. When Shug asks Celie how she imagines God, Celie says, "He big and old and tall and graybearded and white." Shug wants to know why Celie's God looks just like white folks, only bigger; then she admonishes Celie, "You have to git man off your eyeball, before you can see anything at all."[6] Celie is imprisoned by the myths or worldviews of those who have dominated her—men of both races and white people of both sexes. For her to find her way to personal wholeness and mutuality with others, she had to have her sight restored by removal of the cataracts of racist and sexist cultural images and myths.

Lest the Celie example mislead, *myth* should not be relegated to the list of pejorative terms. We live in myth as intimately as we live in our bodies. And while such myths as those that make sense of racism and sexism are sicknesses in need of cures, any fundamental convictions that we live by—often without thinking what they are—are rooted in some myth or worldview. Myths are stories that express a worldview, and they place their inhabitants in a framework of meaning that situates them in relation to images of exemplary human life, to society, to nature, and to whatever gods they trust.

Myths give us our bearings, and they filter our perceptions overwhelmingly. Our myths underlie our morals, and we absorb them with the air we breathe rather than select them after a survey of the options. Religion is basically mythic, and people who grow up in a particular religious setting will always carry the imprint of that ambience even though they may reject that religion and give their allegiance to some other worldview.

Contexts of Moral Vision

Back in the mid-sixties, one brand of contextual ethics was emerging as a counter to moral absolutism. In recognition of the inadequacy of rules to prescribe answers for every decision-making challenge, many ethicists urged that each situation be considered in its uniqueness. Rules could provide guidance, but unusual situations often demanded making exceptions to rules. Joseph Fletcher, the leading exponent of situation ethics or "the new morality" in its inaugural decade, summed up the position by saying, "Love is the only norm."[7] Other principles may guide, but only love is absolute. As the now-Senator John Danforth put it in a sermon to an Episcopalian flock in Saint Louis, "The new morality is like Purina Dog Chow. All you add is love." Danforth was playfully chided for unfair advertising because of his family's interest in Ralston-Purina, but situation ethics took its hardest licks and lashes from other quarters.

Some attacked the relativism of situation ethics by invoking a list of absolutes; they saw little difference between "Love knows best" and "Let your glands be your guide." Others, who also considered themselves contextual ethicists, stressed the setting and circumstance of moral choice, but faulted Fletcher's love as "sloppy agape" and his "situations" as isolated moments in the lives of unconnected individuals. James Gustafson, for one, lamented that "love runs through Fletcher's book like a greased pig" and that his situations lacked scope. He pursued the example of an amorous encounter between two young people alone in a room between 1 A.M. and 3 A.M. after several drinks. Do they see themselves merely as two people who feel sexually attracted to each other? Or do they see themselves as responsible to and for each other over the long haul in a covenantal relationship with a human community to which they are also responsible?[8] In the first instance we have a naked couple in more ways than one; these people are stripped of the histories, the communities, and the plans in which people are appropriately clothed.

In his recent writing in *Ethics from a Theocentric Perspective,* Gustafson further emphasizes the need to see our interactions with each other in the context of larger wholes. As a theological ethicist, he affirms an ultimate context of ordering within which we interact because some ultimate power, some God, impinges on our lives.[9]

Physician Edmund Pellegrino and philosopher Richard Zaner illuminate further the richness of our contexts as they examine what is going on when doctor meets patient.[10] The situation is far more textured and complex than merely being an encounter between a person with medical knowledge and skill and a person with a disease. The doctor comes out of a long Hippocratic tradition of covenantal indebtedness and obligation and works within the current expectations of his profession. Doctors bring to the medical encounter personal moral values, religious beliefs or the functional equivalents, images of doctors and patients, personal and family experiences with disease and illness, fears of death, the slant of specialized training, a political outlook, and more. A patient also brings personal moral values and religious beliefs, images of doctors and patients, anxieties and fears, a personal and family history with health and sickness, a disposition to trust or distrust others, a feeling of financial security or insecurity, and more. Above all, the patient brings an illness— which, as physician Eric Cassell explains, is not the same as a disease.[11] An illness is more than an organic malfunction or infection or injury; it is a web of psychosocial responses to not feeling well— disruptions of relationships, capacities, plans, self-image, and bodily wholeness. "Illness" signals more general disarray than does "disease," and health-care providers can treat the disease without addressing the illness. Both doctor and patient bring to their encounter assumptions about health and illness, and each brings perceptions of the other and perceptions of the other's perceptions.

Beyond the richness and complexity of their interpersonal (and inter-role) meeting, doctor and patient are surrounded by rich and complex contexts. They are surrounded by the claims and concerns of their families. They are surrounded by societal values and expectations and by those of their smaller religious or social circles. They are often surrounded by a hospital or clinic and by other members of the health-care team. They are surrounded by hospital policies, governmental regulations, the demands of third-party payer paperwork, the limitations of law, and the possibilities of malpractice suits. "Where in the world they are" combines with "where they are coming from" to create a deeply layered and richly textured situation. From this perspective, neither patients nor caregivers will be regarded as naked individuals stripped of all historical, social, institutional, and convictional connections. Such an analysis of the physician-patient encounter illustrates what Waldo Beach has called "double contextualism."[12] We decide not only in the context of all the facts of the situation and the various values converging in it but also in the context of the purposes, principles, and outlooks we bring to the situation.

Our contexts are thicker, broader, deeper, and higher than mere "situations," as those have often been perceived. Around and beyond the interpersonal relations of individuals within communities and institutions, our contexts include institutional cultures, policies, roles, and structures. Around and beyond the bare facts of our moral quandaries, our contexts include our universes of discourse—the metaphors, images, and models that shape our interpretations of what is going on in a situation or how a problem is defined. Around and beyond our moments of moral choice, our contexts include our life stories and those of others and also the scripts implicit in our life plans. Around and beyond the moral norms we may invoke to guide or justify an ethical choice, our contexts include worldviews, ideologies, and cultural stories or myths that position us in the larger scheme of things. We inhabit institutional environments. We reside in mythic milieus. We dwell in personal histories. We occupy a universe of order and meaning created by the human imagination just as surely as we occupy a solar system whose existence owes no debt to the human mind.

Ethics of Character in Context

We are attempting to take a good look at the way we see things. We need to review our points of view because we can respond only to what we see. We see only from the vantage points afforded by our historical and social locations and through the lenses afforded by the metaphors, images, myths, and worldviews that filter our experience. William F. May aptly describes ethical theory as "corrective vision."[13] In ethical reflection, we step back from the life of moral development and choice and subject it to critical scrutiny. We do so as the people we have become in the communities and institutions we inhabit, not as detached spectators, but critical reflection can be highly illuminating despite its never being utterly "objective."

The announced focus of our review stamps this endeavor as ethical theory of a particular kind. We are concerned primarily with what makes the persons tick who are interpreting, interacting, evaluating, and deciding. To borrow one of Stanley Hauerwas's titles, "vision and virtue" are two ways of talking about what makes us tick. As we have been saying, vision is a label for the way we look at what is going on. In the words of Bruce Birch and Larry Rasmussen, "Our moral vision is our sense of the total environment in which the moral life is lived."[14] Virtue and character refer to the personal qualities and dispositions that characterize us as we respond to life's challenges and take initiatives in our various social locations and circles of interaction. An ethic of virtue or character need not mean a preoccupation with one's rectitude or a self-centered cultivation of one's goodness. If we understand the self as being a social or relational self, always formed and functioning in connection with others, then virtue and character refer to the typical way we respond to problems, pursue purposes, and relate to other people—not to Benjamin Franklin's checklist of individual moral accomplishments.[15]

This focus on the character of the moral self in its various contexts distinguishes the ethical theory we are following from some other perennial and useful types, but does not imply that those other theories should be discarded.

Some ethical approaches lay primary emphasis on our duties to observe certain moral principles (such as freedom or justice), certain moral rules (such as telling the truth or keeping promises), or certain rights (such as a right to privacy or a right to food). These duties may be viewed as divinely commanded, as rationally self-evident, or as minimally required for orderly societal life, but they are considered obligatory, not because obedience to them will bring desirable consequences or avoid undesirable consequences, but because they are right.

Moral quandaries do not go away because we are people of principle; our principles, rules, or rights may conflict with one another (the mother's right to decide versus the fetus's right to life; honoring the patient's autonomy versus preventing his death). And even if we consider certain rights or rules absolute, we still have to decide whether they apply to the problems we face and, if so, how they do. The distinguishing feature of the ethic of duty is its attempt to determine first and foremost what norm commands obedience in the decision at hand. The approach implies a legal model. We must recognize certain limits within which we can live together in justice and mutual toleration, if not in love.

Another classic type of ethics focuses on ends and consequences. Achieving the good outcome for the person (for instance, happiness or well-being) or the group (for instance, the just society) is the primary aim. Not everyone agrees on the good toward which we should be striving, and when utilitarians pursue the greatest good for the greatest number, we may find reason to object that there are some rights that should not be violated (the right not to be tortured, for instance) no matter how lofty the goals. However, many utilitarians will stand up for minority rights because the possible or known consequences of discrimination are so abhorrent, just as many advocates of meeting obligations regardless of the consequences will do plenty of cost-benefit calculation once the demands of justice have been satisfied or basic human rights have been respected. Agreeing on the weight to give various costs and benefits is a tricky enterprise, but doing cost-benefit analysis is an important aid to ethical decision making.

As H. Richard Niebuhr expressed it in *The Responsible Self,* the first question you ask provides a clue to your fundamental approach. Other approaches are then appropriated within that general orientation. We have said that the ethic of duty asks first which moral law or right obligates us in the situation we face. The ethic of ends and consequences asks what good should be achieved or what bad outcome avoided. To determine an appropriate response, Niebuhr's ethic of responsibility asks first, "What is going on?"[16] How do I interpret what is happening that calls for a response? Decisions about the treatment of a patient, for instance, require a careful reading of the particulars of a complex case in a clinical setting. Citing rules or principles (such as doing no harm or respecting autonomy) and weighing consequences occur in the context of a multifaceted set of circumstances. There are multiple witnesses to call, and there is much circumstantial evidence to consider.

We have been thinking first about taking a good look rather than about getting to a good end or applying the applicable norm. We start with the person who is assessing the situation. A person's outlook includes the principles and values imbedded in the moral traditions of one's communities, but their relevance and appropriateness hinge on a reading of what is going on. What qualities of character dispose you or me to read the situation and to respond in certain characteristic ways? Both the reading and the responding are moral acts. What inclines us to relate to people in typical ways, to react to certain kinds of people in certain kinds of ways, to tilt toward the interests of a particular group, to focus on particular dimensions of a situation? What makes some people walking humane societies, some portable prosecutors, some touring cleanup squads, and others instant spirit-lifters? What qualities of life will cause people to make good decisions on the many occasions when rights and ideals cannot capture the richness and complexity of the challenge? Football coaches sometimes speak of wanting "quality people" at the "skilled positions." In the moral life, every position calls for people of quality.

In addition to focusing on the person faced with ethical choices, our approach calls attention to the fullness of the setting in which the person is interpreting, deciding, and acting. Our surroundings include both the values in the air and the ones in our blood.

A group of metaphors might help delineate the differences in slant or method that we have been sorting out. Traffic lights, including stoplights and caution lights, place us within limits. We are obligated to obey them as a condition for our safety and that of others. They are like principles, rules, or rights protecting human life and well-being. On one hand, headlights and searchlights focus on where we are going. They enable us to see the road to our destination and to read the signs that tell us whether we are headed in the right direction. Floodlights, on the other hand, might help us to see some aspect of a situation that the stoplights and headlights could not illuminate and to expand the reach of the setting we can take in. The eye, "the lamp of the body," enables the "outlook" of the persons who are driving or otherwise seeking to find their way. Headlights, searchlights, and traffic lights are of critical importance, but we have to start with the eyes of the beholders, then move to the lenses and cataracts that correct or distort vision and to the floodlights that bring more things to light.

A Sensible Choice

Have we put too much stock in the sense of sight? To some, seeing seems uninvolved, distant, and too coolly rational. Are we not more in touch with moral dilemmas through feelings and emotions? In *Women's Ways of Knowing*, Belenky, Clinchy, Goldberger, and Tarule object to visual metaphors of knowing, such as illumination, seeing, and light, because they suggest the passivity of a camera capturing something totally separate from it. They convincingly elevate metaphors of voice and silence. In contrast to the eye, they explain, the ear requires closeness. The dialogue of attentive listening and speaking connects people, but seeing suggests removal, separation, and detachment.[17]

The connections these authors want their metaphors to draw actually support the argument of this book in important ways, but more may meet the eye than the authors think. Some ideas of looking might suggest detached objectivity, aloof and unaffected by the pain of others, but that is not the kind of looking and seeing we have in mind. Novelist Flannery O'Connor claims that "the roots of the eye are in the heart." She sees the eye as "an organ which eventually involves the whole personality and as much of the world as can be got into it."[18] The eye, then, is not only "the lamp of the body," which, if healthy, gives light to the whole of it, as Jesus taught; it is the heart's window on the world, the place where one's moral squint first takes effect, the origin of tears. It can make sense to say that the blind "see" and the deaf receive messages.

Not only may our seeing encompass more than the critics allege, but hearing is fraught with some of the same problems that distort and distract seeing. We manage to hear what we want to hear. Others cause us to hear only what they want us to hear. The loudness of some sounds drowns out others. Our location, our cultural conditioning, and the devices we have for transmitting and recording limit and modify what we hear. Language barriers can plague us even when we speak the same native tongue.

We could certainly use other metaphors to "make good sense." The sense of hearing would suggest our ability to listen attentively and empathetically to what people are trying to say and to pick up the moans, cries, and sighs that are too deep for words. We could talk of having a nose for injustice and exploitation; we could focus on our capacity to reach out and touch the isolated and rejected and to allow ourselves to be touched by a helping hand or an entreating one. Seeing, of course, helps us interpret what we hear, locate what we smell, and recognize what is touching us. But the point is not to argue over which metaphor makes the most sense; it is the total person who has a certain moral character and engages in moral action. Seeing involves intellect, will, and emotions; sensing involves seeing, hearing, smelling, and the rest.

A Reversible Order: Behaving Is Also Seeing

Since wanting to see and being willing to see are so important, is it possible that the title of this chapter is turned around? Sometimes we have to put ourselves into a situation before we can see what is going on. Sometimes we have to expose ourselves to others' lives

before we fathom others' needs. It is dangerous to engage in community service or live on a welfare diet for a week or experience a
slum or get to know an AIDS patient because, in doing so, we begin
to see things differently. Our behavior in taking this kind of action is
often prompted by something we have already seen, at least in part,
and may show where our hearts already are. Or we may act out of
curiosity, out of compliance with a school assignment, out of identification with a group of friends, or out of necessity when we happen
to have a flat tire in the wrong place or have to sit next to somebody
on a public conveyance whom we would not otherwise have met.
Out of that behavior, intentional or coincidental, may come revision,
a new outlook. Perhaps that is what Jesus meant when he said, "For
where your treasure is, there will your heart be also" (Matt. 6:21).
Investing can be risky business for our habitual moral vision as well
as for our economic security, especially if maintaining the status quo
is our aim. To behave may also be to see.[19]

We have a circular process on our hands—or is it in our eyes? Our
seeing or our willingness to see may have made the behaving possible, yet behavior may, at times, happen to us as much or more than
we initiate it. More important, if we really want to see, we need to
act on our intentions; otherwise we lose sight of much that we need
to see. If we do not enter into the experience of others, especially
those who are the least advantaged and the most different from ourselves, we shall not only fail to see the world as it is, but we shall also
fail to see ourselves as we are. Therefore, after treating the institutional contexts, the imaginative contexts, and the autobiographical
contexts that we inhabit, this book addresses our need to put ourselves in other people's shoes.

Summary: Professional Ethics in Perspective

Contrary to some individualistic depictions, we are storied, situated, surrounded selves. For us to "do ethics"—to reflect critically
on the character and action of ourselves and our communities—we
must recognize "where in the world we are" and "where we come
from." We abide in personal and cultural stories and in institutions
ranging from the family to the nation and beyond. Our pasts precede
us, our futures lie before us, our cultures surround us, our values
infuse us, our absorbed images shape us, and our myths and
worldviews locate us. We become more ethically perceptive and
sensitive people when we understand ourselves in our layers of contexts and understand what creates and changes those contexts. With
that understanding, we may further complicate the already complicated process of ethical reflection, but we may also better define
some moral problems, clarify some moral conflicts, and even allevi-

ate or head off some moral messes. Looking better could mean doing better.

Many treatments of professional ethics today focus on the standards of behavior expected of people with particular professional roles and responsibilities or on specific ethical quandaries they face as individuals. Without questioning the value of codes and case studies, this treatment of ethics deals with professional ethics from a different perspective. By looking critically at what shapes the outlooks of professionals, as well as people in general, we expand our ethical sensitivity. The way we know is as much a moral matter as the way we choose between alternative actions, and the contexts within which we function are at least as important as the codes we develop and observe. Enlarging the scope of professional ethics moves us beyond the ethics of individuals *in* institutions and professions to the ethics *of* institutions and professions and to the images and myths they embody and transmit.

Because our contexts are multiple and mixed, this book cannot cover them all. Our natural environment, our technological environment, our economic and political systems, and our social classes are some of the contexts that will not receive the attention they deserve. Nevertheless, we view these contexts through our images, metaphors, and worldviews, and the contexts take the shape they take for us because of those lenses. Even the natural world is seen differently by different people as a result of differing worldviews. And it is also in various institutional settings that we experience all of these other contexts.

2
Institutional Contexts: Cultures, Characters, and Professions

The most difficult thing for me to learn is to be hardened but sympathetic, detached but warm. How I admire the interns. How I fear losing my compassion while becoming one of them.

From third-year medicine clerk Sara Jo Friedman's journal

I suspect that this experience can be very destructive to one's self concept, as well as one's perspective of what is happening around one.

From a law student's journal

Any organization of work—industrial, service, blue or white collar—can be described as a *psychostructure* that selects and molds character.

Michael Maccoby, *The Gamesman*

In Wendell Berry's novel *Remembering,* Andy Catlett's whole life has been torn up by the loss of his hand in a corn picker. A general distrust dominates him, and his once-strong relationship with his wife is threatened. He remembers the way it used to be between them:

> It was as though grace and peace were bestowed on them out of the sanctity of marriage itself, which simply furnished them to one another, free and sufficient as rain to leaf. It was as if they were not making marriage but being made by it, and, while it held them, time and their lives flowed over them, like swift water over stones, rubbing them together, grinding off their edges, making them fit together, fit to be together, in the only way that fragments can be rejoined. And though Andy did not understand this, and though he suffered from it, he trusted it and rejoiced in it.[1]

The institution of marriage was larger and stronger than their individual selves, and it had been a means of grace to them. The institution of marriage had sustained them, taught them, bettered them.

A friend of mine gave his testimony to the possibility of edification by institutions as we were driving down the highway toward a committee meeting about the future of ministries in higher education in our region. The meeting would bring my total to two for the year, but it was probably going to jack my companion's total for the week into double digits. He was a denominational executive who had devoted most of his professional life to the processes of creating, maintaining, and reforming the structures of the denomination so that they would reflect the church's message of faith, hope, and love. He admitted with some frustration that most parishioners saw such painstaking attention to process and policy and structure beyond the local level as a regrettable necessity at best and as a pain in the neck at worst. While he viewed the task of attending to the health of the larger institution as a potential means of grace, he doubted that most of the people he served shared that perspective. In fact, even in the ecclesiastical setting, if you have seen one person who thinks committee meetings can be means of grace, you may have seen your last. Keeping the machinery of church governance and mission well oiled is a vocation few covet and most avoid.

Both Berry's narrator and my traveling companion were bucking the tide of popular opinion about institutions. Individualistic Americans find it hard to believe that personal well-being and moral growth can come about because of institutions as well as in spite of them.

In their analysis of the contemporary American character, *Habits of the Heart: Individualism and Commitment in American Life*, Robert Bellah, Richard Madsen, William Sullivan, Ann Swidler, and Steven Tipton found that Americans are beset with the notion that personal happiness and institutional limitations are antithetical. People believe that they must maneuver within institutions to achieve self-fulfillment, but they give scant attention to the management of institutions to enhance personal and societal well-being. They may value marriage and family and perhaps a religious group as rewarding relationships, but they often see these as "life-style enclaves" where one escapes institutional constrictions and the burdens of those different from us, and not as institutions linking people to the past, the future, and the larger society.[2]

Unlike communities where there is an interdependence based on shared history and shared links to public life, life-style enclaves are held together by shared preferences, tastes, and leisure activities that enrich private life and reinforce separation from the larger society.[3] People in such enclaves gauge the value of these associations by the level of good feelings they generate. If their participants begin to feel a sense of interdependence that is more important than

immediate personal emotional payoffs, a sense of history that is
more far-reaching than recent shared experiences, and a sense of
connection that is more encompassing than the membership of the
enclave, then a community has emerged. And a community has
value as an institution that is greater than the immediate returns that
individuals are getting on their emotional investments.

Our Institutional Habitats

For better and for worse, institutions surround us and saturate us.
Dictionaries inform us that any significant or established practice, relationship, or organization in a society is an institution. Therefore we can
call both monogamy and prostitution institutions. The local merchants'
Christmas parade and the homecoming dance are institutions. Both
legal and illegal activities and organizations may be institutions. We are
born into them; we are educated in them; we work in them; we come
home to them. Through them, we participate in government; we receive
and give medical care; we worship; we serve others; others serve us.

In his analysis of human development, Erik Erikson emphasizes
the importance of institutional support for the successful negotiation
of the eight stages of the life cycle that he delineates. In order for
infants to learn basic trust, parental figures must provide an environment that can be trusted, and, as children mature, they will need
ways to express that trust institutionally—for example, through pro-
ductive work, religion, and social action. The next challenge for the
child is to learn autonomy to counteract shame and doubt. This combination of self-control and self-esteem trickles down from parents
whose autonomy and self-reliance have been fostered in political
and economic institutions that empower them.

For children to learn to take initiative and avoid crippling guilt,
their play stage needs the support of a family and family surrogates
who value the children for who they are rather than what they do.
For them to become industrious and not feel inferior at the fourth
stage depends on a school, neighborhood, and child-care environment where they work side by side with other children in an encour-
aging institutional setting.

Gaining a sense of personal identity in adolescence requires a social milieu where constructive peer-group activity is available,
where role models embody ideals that deserve allegiance, and
where leaders do not advance to their positions through corruption
and sheer exercise of power. Development of capacities for intimacy
and solidarity in young adulthood depends on an undergirding institutional balance of work and stable, loving relationships, such as
friendship and marriage. Supportive institutional settings of competition and cooperation make a powerful difference.

The last two crises in psychosocial development challenge us to "generativity" rather than self-absorption and stagnation, and to integrity rather than despair. In the first, we start something new; we bring into being children, homes, ideas, and enterprises, and we nurture them. In the last, we are challenged to accept the life we have lived and the legacy we are leaving and to face not being around any more. In both cases, institutional outlets and supports—family, work, interest groups, membership in religious communities, and civic involvements—are essential. From first to last, Erikson's theory teaches us to appreciate the crucial place of institutional settings in personal development.[4]

The Nature of Institutions

For much of our discussion, the terms *institution* and *organization* could be used interchangeably, but Philip Selznick makes a useful distinction between an organization and an institution: "Organizations become institutions as they are infused with value, that is, prized not as tools alone but as sources of direct personal gratification and vehicles of group identity."[5] Such value-bearing organizations as corporations, schools, hospitals, social service agencies, churches, and governmental agencies, and the professions and occupations whose members staff them are the institutions that will concern us as contexts of ethics in this chapter. Both our organizations and our occupations are places within which to be and places from which to see. They are both points of contact with moral questions and points of view for moral insight.

Being part of such institutions is part of being human, and healthy institutions enhance our human possibilities rather than blight them. It has often been argued that religious movements lose their way when they become institutionalized, but if groups and practices are to persist through the years, they have to become organized and institutionalized. Groups do not become questionable by becoming institutions.

Institutions have a life of their own. They are more than the sum of the selves who make them up. Social realists believe that "society is as real as individuals."[6] Radical individualism, by contrast, always considers the individual the primary reality and views society and its organizations and institutions only as combinations of individuals. Ours is a different claim. The organizations and professions that provide the settings of our daily endeavors have traditions, values, styles of operation, and tendencies that are not reducible to those brought by the individuals who make them up. Granted that these institutions would be nothing without the people who create and populate them and that they are in constant flux because of the initiative and acquiescence of people, we fool ourselves if we do not recognize the conditioning power they exert—a power that often is not the overt or conscious intention of any one person or group.

A friend of mine who teaches at another institution of higher education once bemoaned to me some conditions on his campus, but then said reassuringly, "But it's hard to kill a good college." He was saying that traditions, constituencies, structures, human and material resources, stories, values, and goals were at work in the life of his school, and these were not going to be demolished or permanently eroded by the poor judgment or myopic vision of a few individuals. In a similar vein, Robert Wright, acting editor of the *New Republic*, concluded his extremely negative assessment of the legacy of President Reagan in this way: "The fact that things worked out no worse than they did is either a tribute to the institutional sturdiness of the presidency or proof of the existence of God."[7]

For an example of institutional influences on the down side, we can cite the persistent drag of what is often called systemic or institutional racism, sexism, classism, and ageism. Although the current decision-makers in an institution may be open to the full participation of people of all races, sexes, income levels, and ages, the residue of past patterns in the institution and in the larger society that surrounds it may perpetuate certain levels of corporate management as all-male clubs, certain schools as the habitats of the white and the privileged, and certain positions as the bailiwicks of the under fifty-five. Theologians have labeled such isms as social sin. As Letty Russell says, social sin has a life of its own. "It functions in social systems in such a way that people are battered and dehumanized in countless ways simply because society does business-as-usual."[8]

Traditions, assumptions, stereotypes, and social climates do not change overnight; it usually takes sustained, concerted initiatives to counteract the drift that may be subtly present in application forms, qualifying examinations, publicity, job definitions, recruiting strategies, and work environment. Affirmative action programs, which can include strategies ranging from seeking applicants from the previously under-represented group to setting quotas to assure acceptable results, aim at reversing entrenched institutional or systemic discrimination.

Another example of the dangers of institutional drag is the temptation for us to devote total loyalty to an institution, especially when the institution stands for noble ideals and becomes the chief or only definer of a person's identity. In such cases, loyalty to the institution quickly becomes idolatrous. The institution is vested with the god-like prerogative to define what is good and right. The institutional role consumes us. We lose ourselves in our work. When we become so committed to one institution, either voluntarily or involuntarily, that it becomes the total definer of our personhood, we have become "institutionalized."

When ethical values become institutionalized in the life of an organization, it is a sign of institutional health, but when a person becomes institutionalized, it is a sign of illness. "Involuntary commitment" to an institution is sometimes necessary as a temporary measure for the acutely mentally ill, but forcible commitment of those who are not sufficiently institutionalized into the reigning societal ideology for the purpose of indoctrination or mind control is a form of torture.

In *Moral Man and Immoral Society*, Reinhold Niebuhr drives home a warning about disguised selfishness in devotion to social groups.[9] What would seem highly questionable to me if I were doing it solely for my own aggrandizement and gain can appear justifiable and even honorable to me if I am doing it for my nation, my company, my college, my family, my political party, my church, my team, my social organization, or my friends.

In his book *Where the Law Ends* Christopher Stone recalls the Equity Funding Insurance Company scandal.[10] The company had been reporting $3 billion of life insurance in force, but $2 billion of that amount was bogus. Policies had been written on nonexistent people and sold to other companies to bring in needed cash. Finally, it took the entire organization to deceive the auditors, stockholders, and policy purchasers. The scheme was known in the company as "the Y business" or "department 99." It became a joke, a game involving after-hours parties to forge fictitious policies. Loyal employees did on behalf of the company what they probably would have had more difficulty justifying had they been acting on self-interest alone. The other side of the argument can readily cite such insider trading tycoons as Ivan Boesky who seem to be unabashed adherents to the creed enunciated by Michael Douglas in the movie *Wall Street*: "Greed is great. Greed is good. Greed works."

The demands of roles that we are assigned in institutions may corrupt as badly as our uncritical loyalty to them does. Roles can give us leave to dehumanize others or to deprecate ourselves. Philip Zimbardo's experiment at Stanford University in 1971 assigned one group of people to serve as guards over another group who were designated as prisoners. The results were highly disturbing. The twenty-four young men who were assigned roles as either prisoners or guards were all normal, emotionally stable, intelligent, and middle class. They had neither criminal records nor prison experience. Yet in the first day, the guards were already treating the prisoners in brutal and callous ways, and the prisoners were already meek, subservient, and unmotivated to exercise their open option to leave the experiment. Some had to be released during the first four days due to hysteria and depression. So frightening were the results that the experiment was terminated after six days.[11] This experience gives booming testimony to the moral significance of defining and assuming roles. We enter them at considerable risk to ourselves and others.

Roles are not sinister just because they can be seductive. Roles can keep us in line and prompt us to discharge obligations that we might otherwise neglect. Roles can facilitate communication, helpfulness, and productivity. They can cause us to grow in response to their demands. We all fulfill roles by sheer necessity and by the common grace of life in community. It is a mistake to make neat distinctions between the real person and the person's roles. Our combinations and renditions of roles make us the unique persons we are, not our shedding of all roles. Stripped of all roles, we become denuded of the connectedness and relatedness that are crucial to personal identity. We find ourselves in communities and institutions, and the life of communities and institutions requires some definition and discharge of roles. Defining moral responsibility in institutional life requires attention to the implications of moral imperatives for specific roles.[12]

A major reason why organizations and institutions are often viewed as either morally neutral or morally negative is that, as they grow larger and become more systematic about the pursuit of their ends, they inevitably become more bureaucratic. Bureaucracies tend to be hierarchical, specialized, and impersonal. Roles narrow, paperwork proliferates, and layers pile up in the name of efficiency. The personal touch may get lost in the process. Peter Lenrow, who writes about social-service agencies, sees bureaucracies as being so geared toward efficiency that they always operate at cross-purposes with the aims of the helping professional.[13] He has located a problem, but one hopes he has not sealed a fate.

Bureaucracies often do put barriers in the way of creativity and innovation, and they may strain people through the sieve of standard operating procedures and finely differentiated roles and functions. Nevertheless, it is equally true that structures, systems, standard procedures, institutional chains of command, and policy constraints can be formidable inhibitors of irresponsibility and abuse of power. In making this very point, William F. May allows that bureaucratic structures will not take an institution to new heights of vision and creativity, but that they can do much to insure at least a minimal level of fairness and accountability. Writing about hospitals, he states: "Moral purposes must be largely built into the very structure of the institution. Management must oversee this task of moral construction. It cannot depend upon the fitful efforts of individual persons alone to keep covenant."[14]

The Cultures and Characters of Institutions

At the head of the chapter is a statement by Michael Maccoby about organizations of work being psychostructures that select and mold character. This claim plunges us into the discussions of organizational or corporate "culture" that have gained increasing prominence in the past decade. To give a specific example of Maccoby's generalization, we can cite this description of the Norton Company found in *Corporate Ethics: A Prime Business Asset,* published by The Business Roundtable in 1988: "Talk with Norton people or other business people who are familiar with Norton, and the portrait of the Company is remarkably consistent: a straightlaced, trustworthy, extremely upright organization which seems to attract and promote straightlaced, trustworthy, extremely upright people."[15] The company not only has a culture; it has a character. As Charles McCoy explains, to say it has character emphasizes "the intentional element" of corporate culture.[16] If a corporation can be committed to values and shape the future in accord with them, it has a character.

In *Organizational Culture and Leadership,* Edgar H. Schein has provided no less than seven definitions of organizational culture from the massive literature on the subject: observed behavioral regularities in the interaction of members; norms in a working group; dominant values that the organization espouses; the philosophy that guides organizational policy; the rules or "ropes" for succeeding in the organization; the emotional climate conveyed by the physical environment and social interaction; and his own definition—"basic assumptions and beliefs that are shared by members."[17] Schein considers the other elements he lists to be reflections of the most basic foundations of the culture—the shared assumptions and beliefs. In answer to the question, What is culture? I am inclined to say, all of the above. Culture is an inclusive term, but our discussion will focus on the way of life that pervades the organization or institution. The basic values or beliefs that guide the culture at either the conscious or unconscious level might be termed the "character" of the culture.

Perhaps an illustration will help clarify the meaning of corporate culture. Douglas Sturm did an ethical assessment of the Sun Company that revealed a high level of employee anxiety over a transition in the identity or character or culture of the company. The old Sun had been paternalistic, familial, benignly dictatorial, tightly integrated, centralized, medium sized, highly personal in leadership style, people oriented, and topped by a family-controlled board. The new Sun—which a merger, an acquisition, and a change in chief executive officers helped to produce—was more managerial than paternalistic, more professional than familial, more diversified, larger, more remote in leadership style, tilted toward self-initiated employee development instead of centrally directed programs, governed by a board composed increasingly of outsiders, and more capital intensive. These two styles exalted different values, set different priorities, and created different cultures. Employees who felt secure in one culture were faced with major adjustment or a move to a company where they felt more at home.[18]

Organizations and institutions have traditions, systems of decision making, priorities, characteristic channels of communication, senses of mission, momentums, values, and stories and heroes that perpetuate and embody those values. They attract, select, reward, and enhance the influence of certain kinds of people. This mix of factors gives the institution its culture, its character, its distinctive ethos. That character, which is created by the people who are active in the organization's formation and development, becomes bigger than the combination of the members' individual characters and continually shapes those who work in its orbit. Schein does not feel that the importance of the ability to influence an organization's culture can be overemphasized: "There is a possibility—underemphasized in leadership research—that the *only thing of real importance that leaders do is create and manage culture* and that the unique talent of leaders is their ability to work with culture."[19] If he is even close to the truth, and if ethics is concerned about institutions, cultures rate close attention.

To view a corporation as having a culture and a character is to reject the claim that we should not expect moral responsibility of an organization structured to fashion a product as efficiently as possible.[20] A corporation is more than a machine or a neutral structure; it is a moral agent.[21] To address life in corporations and other such institutions, we must deal with more than the moral choices of individuals within institutions; we must learn to assess the moral import and impact of the culture and character of the institution—what effects it has on people within it, on the communities around it, on all of the "stakeholders" (a term I first saw in the literature of Cummins Engine Company) who interact with it, and on the environment that undergirds and surrounds it. For that reason, McCoy stresses the difference between corporate ethics or the ethics of organizations and the ethics of individuals.[22] For that reason, the Boeing Company posits as one of its principles, "Ethics should be approached as a systems issue and not as a problem of 'bad' individuals."[23]

An institutional culture or ethos may be exemplified in such superficial observances as men with three-piece suits and no facial hair and women wearing suits in order to comply with the preferences of the CEO. But culture covers many dimensions of an organization's ethos that are of moral moment—images of the good employee, breadth of participation in decision making, channels of communication into and within the company, the way rewards are distributed, the depth of concern for employees, definition of the company's mission, and attitudes toward "stakeholders"—customers, creditors, the community, the government, the environment, and so on. These indicators provide a better measure of a company's responsibility than corporate codes of ethics and philanthropic contributions.

In some corporations, corporate responsibility is a department or a cluster of public relations programs or a code of prohibited behaviors. In others, ethics affects the full range of corporate activities—training of new employees, decisions about which projects to finance, arrangement of office space, processes of decision making, plant closures and locations, and assessments of environmental impact.

Just as you have not seen all business corporations if you have seen one, you also have not seen all colleges or hospitals or service agencies if you have seen one. They differ in culture and character. Institutions of higher education, for instance, display great variation in the percentage of athletes who graduate, the hours professors spend advising, and the opportunities students have to participate in institutional governance. Different student bodies take academic dishonesty, vandalism, and emotional problems of hallmates with differing degrees of seriousness. Various Greek organizations, theatrical groups, and athletic teams also have their own distinctive cultures, which have predictable effects on students who join them.

Hospitals also have cultures and characters. Even parts of hospitals do. Transplant units may surround patients and families with psychiatrists, nutritionists, rehabilitation therapists, social workers, chaplains, and ethicists, or they may focus more narrowly on the surgical procedure and on the legal protections to which both surgeon and patient are entitled. Some intensive-care units have individual rooms to preserve privacy instead of amphitheater arrangements to enhance efficiency, and some locate all electrical outlets on one side of the bed so that loved ones can have access to patients on the other side. Their policies may or may not maintain open visiting hours as long as some medical procedure is not going on, emphasize patient autonomy and family participation in decision making, and provide interdisciplinary consultation—including psychiatrists, social workers, and ethicists. Intensive-care units are structured and run differently and therefore have different values and priorities built into their settings and policies. Provisions for more sensitive care do not eliminate the highly stressful experience that patients, families, and health-care professionals endure in ICUs, but they do help, and they both reflect institutional values and affect personal ones.

The ability to clarify and shape the values underlying the culture and character of an institution has broad ramifications. We can ex-

amine the culture of an entire corporation or of a particular division
or plant. We can assess the culture of an entire denomination or
religious body or of a local congregation; of an entire university or
of a school or office in it; of an entire hospital or of a service within
it; of an entire student body or of a subgroup within it; of a school
system or of a school or of a band or team.

Even a family has a culture and a character. A family stands for
certain things, and its members either react and rebel against the
values and priorities that reside in family tradition, story, and example, or embrace and embody them. Reinhold Niebuhr liked to tell a
story to illustrate that grace moves not only through persons to institutions but also through social institutions to persons. A wealthy
industrialist who had clawed his way to the top woke up one day to
discover that his particular entrepreneurial style had become socially unacceptable, especially to his family. His wife and daughters
did not like what they were hearing about him, and they began to
ask embarrassing questions at the dinner table. In order to look better in their eyes, he hired a public relations expert to improve his
image (not to change his character). Over his initial objections, the
PR man convinced him that he would need to sponsor some community charities, feign interest in the well-being of his employees, and
change some of the ruthless practices he used against his competitors. An amazing thing happened. The man began to like what he
was pretending to be. He became transformed by his efforts to appear different. The individual was "graced" by institutional pres-
sures.[24] Behaving differently led to seeing differently.

Governing Bodies as Institutions

A legislature does not fit neatly into our analysis of organizational
culture and character. There is overlap, however. The more representatives to a governing body give the task of governing their full-
time attention, the more the body develops a culture; and even
bodies that meet periodically accumulate traditions and work within
structures that give a particular character to the enterprise.

The institutional responsibility of legislators deserves special mention, not because of these similarities to the institutions we have
been considering, but because of a distinctive form of institutional
irresponsibility that plagues legislatures. As David Price, now a
member of the U.S. House of Representatives from North Carolina,
and Richard Fenno have alleged, legislators tend to accentuate their
personal ties with the electorate and downplay their responsibility
for making the legislature work well as an institution. They would
rather be able to say they voted for one of the many versions of an
ethics bill that never got passed during the legislative session than to

invest themselves in the arduous process of producing the best bill with enough votes to pass it into law. They would rather be able to say they voted against taxes or for across-the-board reductions than to struggle to determine which programs best serve the public good and what revenues are required to do what needs to be done. They often run "against the government" and try to distance themselves from their fellow legislators rather than take responsibility for what Fenno calls "the collective performance of Congress."[25]

For a member of a representative governing body, getting serious about institutional ethics means doing more than being an honest and industrious legislator; it means learning how to make the system work to make its greatest possible contribution to the public good. If winning the next election blinds representatives to concerns other than the image they project to voters, our legislative institutions will fail to fulfill the purposes for which they were created.

Professions as Institutions

Not only are the organizations within which we work institutional contexts of ethics; so are the professions within which we practice. People's perceptions of themselves and the situations they encounter are profoundly shaped by the preparation they receive to pursue a particular occupation. And we practice our professions within the expectations and standards of our peers as well as within the structures of organizations.

The argument over who gets to wear the badge of "the professional" is one we shall leave to others. Historically, "the professions"—law, medicine, teaching, and the ministry—were distinguished from business, for instance, because of differences in educational requirements, standards of entry, and obligation to public service. Today nursing endeavors to upgrade its professional status by "differentiated practice" to distinguish those who are trained in two-year associate's programs or hospital programs from those with bachelor's and graduate degrees. The helping professions become an ever-larger umbrella. Business management, engineering, journalism, and accounting become more self-consciously professional. And the list goes on.

Trying to restrict the ranks of professionals to a limited number of occupations is a fruitless and needless venture, but raising the sights of all occupations to see the calling of the professional is a crucial task. In *Habits of the Heart,* Bellah and his colleagues bemoan the nineteenth-century shift from understanding a profession as a calling to seeing it as a career. As a calling, a profession traditionally involved taking up a defined role in the life of the larger community; as a career a profession became primarily a means to personal advancement.[26] As a mere career the profession is not one's link to community, but a ladder to personal success.

The authors of *Habits of the Heart* want management (which plays an increasingly dominant role in American life) to return to professionalism in the old sense. Standards of competence are not to be disparaged, but standards of public obligation must be given greater emphasis. What is widely referred to as "the social responsibility of the corporation" should become "a constitutive structural element in the corporation itself" instead of a "kind of public relations whipped cream decorating the corporate pudding." For such a transformation to occur, business ethics will have to receive a central place in the education of managers.[27]

The manager's professional formation in business school is typical of the socialization that takes place in all professional education. A person sees the world differently and has a different self-concept because of what James Elkins calls "the initiation and rites of passage that one undergoes to become a 'professional.'" Although he writes about legal education, Elkins's insights have broad application. "The person stands in a different place to view the same world."[28] Budding professionals feel new power and prestige, analyze situations with a new set of tools, and speak with a new vocabulary. These students have gained something in the process, but Elkins also finds in the journals of law students a sense of loss. A human reaction to a wreck is displaced by a legal reaction. Students speak of acquiring a one-track mind. From his studies of fourteen law students, James C. Foster finds a "depoliticizing" process at work in legal education. Even for those who viewed the profession as a way to become more able to change an unjust society and protect human rights, law school tends to privatize law as a means to achieve personal goals and to depoliticize the lawyers so that they become uncritical buttresses of the system. You learn to play a game in which there is no right or wrong.[29] As Elkins summarizes, "The world viewed through a legal prism is a narrowly constructed one of rights and duties, privileges and powers. It is a world which reduces the experience of and with people to judicial opinions which substitute for first-hand experience."[30] A law student told me recently that when she objected to a certain practice as being unethical during a discussion in her class on contracts, the professor responded, "You will take ethics next year."

To continue the visual metaphor, we can add Wendell Berry's lament about "one-eyed specialties."[31] He is indicting contemporary American education in general rather than law schools in particular. In the "compartmental structure of the universities," he finds that "mutually sustaining and enriching disciplines are divided, according to 'professions,' into fragmented, one-eyed specialties." The professors of law are solely responsible for law, the college of agriculture for farming, the philosophy department for morality, and the political science department for government, yet all of us have a vital stake in all of them.

In another objection to the effects of legal education, the critical legal-studies movement argues that the law is far from neutral, rational, and scientific, as the legal establishment likes to pretend; it is instead shot through with political bias in favor of the wealthy and powerful. Every profession should look at itself with a similar critical agenda. What economic and political forces threaten to domesticate the profession so that it becomes an accomplice in the perpetuation of unjust social systems and structures? Paulo Freire has alerted us to the fact that no education is politically neutral.[32] Even literacy training is politically loaded either as a bulwark to the status quo or as a force for change.

The testimony from medical students gives as much pause as the journals of law students. From a student's fear of losing compassion in the process, expressed in the quotation at the beginning of the chapter, to a professor of surgery's labeling of medical training as "a hazing rite," it is not a pretty story. At worst, medical school produces testimony like this:

> One thing medical training does is smash your ideals and take away your niceness as a person. The hours that you work, the years of deprivation, being treated like a piece of dirt by everyone, being put under all this stress and pressure and nobody cares, and nobody thinks of you as a human being. You become an automaton doing things for the big guys.
>
> I know a lot of really good people who came out of their training being not as good or as caring as when they went in. All the years of deprivation make some of them reach a point where they come into their own and think they deserve all they get. I've seen that happen to people, and when it does, there's no charity anymore.[33]

People will argue that compassion cannot be taught to people in their mid-twenties, but surely it can be encouraged rather than discouraged by the training doctors receive. One of my former students reported being told by a medical-school professor as they made rounds, "Never touch the patient." In another medical school, the attending physician touched gangrenous limbs that no student in his entourage wanted to handle and then said to his charges as they walked down the hall, "Always touch the patient." I have to believe that the difference between those two role models made a difference in their students, although my former student was proud of the fact that he continued to sneak in the touches despite what the professor said.

As in the case of legal training, students in medical school gain much to make them more effective and useful in medical school, but do they have to lose as much as they often do in the process? If it turns out that their professional education makes them more inclined to treat organs and diseases than to care for people, more skilled at reading CT scans but less able and willing to listen to patients' complaints, and more dependent on various actors on the health-care team but less respectful of the voice that fellow team members should have in decisions about patient care, the gains are overshadowed by the losses and lacks.

Maccoby's saying that organizations of work are psychostructures that select and mold character is equally applicable to professional education. Certain images of the good doctor or nurse or lawyer or manager or journalist or engineer or teacher perpetuate themselves through the selection and socialization processes of professional school.

Nurses' education provides an apt example. The traditional nurse was the "yes-woman," and the preparation process tended to weed out "uppity" types who did not defer unquestioningly to the physicians' judgment. In response to this assertion, a physician friend has cited situations he has encountered in which nurses ran wards or floors which such authority that no physician would cross them, but I am referring to a general historical tendency that is under increasing challenge today. The Great Depression contributed mightily to the subordination of nurses by pushing them from more independent public-health positions to the staffs of hospitals, which had previously been filled by students. Now, among the newer breed of nurses, we find patient advocates determined to express the concerns of the patients whom they care for and nurse practitioners performing many functions formerly reserved for physicians. In the top intensive-care units, nurses know more about how to operate medical machines and monitors than most doctors do. They know more about how to resuscitate a patient, set a respirator, and watch a respirator. If and when arguments arise about whether another patient can be added over the stated capacity of the unit, these nurses may protest about dilution of the quality of care. Although some physicians still demean nurses and some nurses still feel more comfortable in a subservient role, the new nurse is no "yes-person." A profession is changing and demanding to be paid in accordance with its importance; as a result, hospitals, nursing homes, and other institutional contexts of health care are changing.

The professional preparation of academics is also profoundly influential. The graduate training of college and university professors has produced the narrow disciplinary specialization that dominates educational purpose and curricular structure in contemporary higher education. People schooled in increasingly narrow technical slices of segregated fields of study pay scant attention to integration of knowledge, value presuppositions and conflicts in their disciplines, and relationships between the material in a course and citizenship in a democratic society. In such an environment, institutional politics easily sinks to departmental protection of turf. Many of the curricular reforms that are currently being inaugurated are aimed at correcting these very problems.

The debate about the morality of the way we learn has been presented recently as a contrast between "separated" and "connected" knowing. The authors of *Women's Ways of Knowing* describe connected knowing as collaborative, question posing, dialogical, and empathetic. Partners listen to each other on the other's terms. Authority resides in shared experience rather than in the status and power of those with credentials as experts. Connected knowing views the author and the position or work of the author together. In contrast, separated knowers keep their distance from the subject matter to see it "objectively." They believe that connecting a person with a position distorts perception. Learning is individual mastery, not a collaborative search.[34]

Parker Palmer, writing in *Change* magazine, calls "objectivism" what those authors label "separated knowing." It holds the world at arm's length from the knower, analytically chops the objects of knowledge into smaller and smaller pieces, and moves the pieces around as the knower sees fit. (Do you remember the answer to the question about who the strongest person in the world is? The answer is: an intellectual because of the intellectual's ability to hold the weightiest matters at arm's length forever.) Epistemology and ethics are inseparable; our way of knowing implies a way of living. Like Belenky and her colleagues, Palmer sees this objectivism spawning a competitive individualism that destroys community. We want to dominate more than cooperate because we have a dominating approach to knowledge.[35] Thus we have yet another rendition of "seeing is behaving." When we realize that our educations cause us to see the world in a particular way, subjecting our ways of knowing to critical scrutiny becomes a moral imperative.

Different professionals bring the traditions, codes, slants, and concerns of their professional contexts into the organizational contexts of corporations, hospitals, universities, governmental agencies, and church bureaucracies. They also develop and practice as professionals within the contexts of political and economic systems. They may find in the process that the expectations of their institutional roles and the system may grate against the canons of the profession.

The corporate lawyer may find it difficult at times to serve two masters—the law and the corporation—and maintain personal integrity. The physician or nurse may feel a conflict between hospital policy, insurance company policy, or governmental policy and professional oath. For an extreme case, consider the physicians who were called in to examine and treat the political prisoners who were tortured and killed in South African or Chilean detention centers. Journalists may be torn between managing news and uncovering news or between selling papers or magazines or scooping other channels and waiting to check out the story. Engineers may have to struggle with meeting environmental standards in governmental regulations or pleasing superiors by avoiding costly adjustments when no one, probably, will ever know the difference. Military chaplains may get in a bind between the demands of being a good organization person and the needs of members of the military. University professors may wonder how institutional expectations should be weighed against scholarly dedication.

Once the professional leaves the institutional context of professional education, there may be considerable choice about the institutional context of one's practice. It makes a difference whether you are a professor, a dean, or a department chair in a small liberal arts college or in a large research university. It makes a difference whether you are a physician in a small-town practice, a health-maintenance organization, a clinic mainly serving Medicaid patients, or a university medical center. It makes a difference whether you are a lawyer in an organization that defends only people who have received the death penalty, a firm that concentrates on environmental issues, a large corporation, a governmental agency, a legal-aid office, or a generalized partnership in a small town. It is not true that if you have seen one lawyer, doctor, or professor, you have seen them all. Different institutional contexts and different payrolls attract different people and do different things to them.

The sign on the old, unpaved country road read, "Choose your rut carefully; you will be in it for the next fifteen miles." Something similar should be written over the door of any educational institution. The "rut" we choose influences us powerfully. A college student once complained to me that it was unfair for our college to require students to take a religion course. He said, "That's tampering with my life." I hastened to point out that his life was being tampered with in every course he took. If it was not, I contended, he was wasting his money because he certainly was not getting an education. Any education worth its salt tampers with our lives. An honest educational institution will strive to be self-conscious and self-critical about the values that inform its tampering. The wise student will go into the process with eyes wide open.

In recent years, such scandals as Watergate, "Iran-Contra-gate," and insider-trading revelations have triggered widespread concern about the character of the people our schools turn out. One laudable response has been the inauguration of ethics courses in more professional schools, but that strategy falls far short of adequately addressing the problem. A good ethics course will improve moral reasoning ability and make people more adept at analyzing and supporting moral claims. It may even enrich the students' moral imagination and raise their consciousness of the ethical frontiers of a profession or a society, but it cannot guarantee personal integrity, fairness, or compassion.

Some argue that little or no morality gets learned beyond the age of ten and that college is not apt to compensate for what did not happen at the parental knee. While it would be hard to over-emphasize the importance of the early years in the molding of character, this claim underestimates the moral import of a person's total experience in higher education. Values are embedded in the curriculum as a whole (not just the ethics courses), the role models pass on the traditions of liberal learning and the professions, and interaction with one's peers advances the socialization process. These and other aspects of life in educational institutions shape a person's ethical outlook, enlarge or constrict the world in which a person consciously functions, and encourage or discourage the cultivation of certain virtues or qualities of life. Educational institutions should not be endeavoring to program uniform moral products, but they should be self-conscious about the effects of the total life of the institution on the sort of people the students and the employees are becoming.

Summary

As people who are constantly living our versions of morality, we live in institutions and institutions live in us. These institutional contexts are both points of contact and points of view for the moral life. Moral development is not a private enterprise; it occurs in community. Moral responsibility includes being responsible persons within institutions; it also means making our institutions more responsible. To make better institutions, we need to understand the values that reside in organizational cultures and professions and the moral consequences of exposure to these institutions. We must also learn how systems, structures, cultures, and institutional character can be changed.

We leave to the next chapter a discussion of what makes some institutional structures and purposes more ethical in practice than others. This chapter will have accomplished its aim if it has heightened awareness of both the stubbornness of systemic evils and the promise of uplifting institutional environments. It has significantly expanded the context of our ethical efforts if it has provided a counterpoint to the notion of persons existing *in* but not *with* institutions. We may not be more ethical because we perceive our settings and situations differently, but we just might be less naïve, apathetic, and ineffective in relating our moral commitments to the social world we inhabit.

3
Institutional Contexts: Levels, Covenants, and Callings

The Business Roundtable entitled its 1988 publication on ethics *Corporate Ethics: A Prime Business Asset,* and the introduction to its survey of the notable endeavors of several corporations to bring ethics into the very heart of their operations carries the assertion that "corporate ethics is a strategic key to survival and profitability in this era of competitiveness in a global economy."[1] There is a vast difference between this faith that ethics and success will go hand in hand and the cynicism of Trudeau's Phil Slackmeyer, pictured opposite, who reduced ethics to "a powerful negotiating tool" and served time in prison for insider trading. Nevertheless, reducing corporate ethics to a strategy for success is a mistake no matter what form it takes. It goes without saying that fiscal profitability is essential to a corporation's survival, but concern about institutional morality should not merely be a function of concern for institutional success understood in monetary terms.

Doing good and doing well may often overlap considerably, but several of the companies featured in *Corporate Ethics* have taken actions dictated by their company ethic that could have had negative effects on their profits. There was no guarantee that recalling Tylenol would benefit Johnson and Johnson, that withdrawing Riviton and Fruit Roll-ups would benefit General Mills, or that the standards GTE adopted concerning payments abroad would not prove costly to the company. Chemical Bank might have prospered financially by doing business with massage parlors or pornographers or by financing arms exports or corporate raiding. Yet it has eschewed all these involvements. Morally sensitive management will not always outdo the competition, but some companies have decided that some practices are wrong even if they are lucrative.

Advocates of institutional moral responsibility should be searching for norms that are based on some other rationale than institutional self-interest conceived in terms of profitability, but, in a pluralistic society, what measures of institutional moral responsibility can we use? What values and norms should guide an institution's ethic? Who should decide what values and norms should guide an institution's life? How can institutions be shaped to reflect those guides if and when we can agree on them?

Layers of Institutional Control

One approach to institutional responsibility is the fence approach. Concentric circles of social control keep the institution within the bounds of propriety as defined by the larger society outside the institution and the leadership inside the institution. Law, public opinion, and management draw the lines within which the institution and its employees are expected to function. The reigning assumption is that institutions respond best to legal limits and societal pressure. Make the rules and penalties clear, and people will know their limits.

The outer circles or fences include those forms of regulation and limitation that are imposed on an institution by some government-designated or self-appointed representative of the larger society to make it contribute to the public good, or at least to prevent its doing great harm. Civil and criminal law and the regulations and guidelines of the Occupational Safety and Health Administration, the Environmental Protection Agency, the Internal Revenue Service, the Equal Employment Opportunity Commission, the Interstate Commerce Commission, and the Securities and Exchange Commission are examples of these outer rings of constraint. Divestitures of stocks, boycotts, and demonstrations also exert influence from outside. Professional codes of conduct may hold an individual in a particular workplace accountable to professional peers outside that particular workplace who have an interest in protecting the reputation as well as the economic security and political clout of the profession. Shareholder resolutions and union activity have both outside and inside features. The people involved are taking an adversarial stance, but they have a direct economic interest in the institution.

These external constraints may demand certain results (for instance, required environmental impact statements and hiring guidelines or quotas). They may protect rights by requiring plant closing notices, nondiscriminatory hiring, access for the handicapped, or protection against harassment. They may broaden participation in decision making. Christopher Stone, for instance, has advocated the introduction of a certain number of government-appointed corporate directors in corporations holding a large market share of particular products or companies whose operations and products have a telling impact on some public good such as environmental quality.[2]

These external impositions of limits have much to commend them. They use public representatives to interpret the public good. They avoid naïve trust in institutional self-transformation. They set limits to institutional irresponsibility.

Their inadequacies, however, are equally impressive. With the fence approach, the moral is often reduced to the legal, and demands deal mainly with what is most objectionable and most enforceable from outside. It is impossible to regulate and prescribe everything of moral consequence even if it were desirable, and it probably is not. Regulators may be tempted by co-option or rendered irrelevant by isolation. Outside agencies are notoriously uneven in the will and ability to enforce standards of institutional rectitude. What they know depends heavily on the cooperation of those being regulated, and the line between chilliness and coziness is a tightrope.

Of much greater moment for the moral seriousness of the institution are internal constraints or regulations—corporate codes of conduct, institutional review boards (which are sometimes externally mandated), ethics committees, ethics consultants, ethics offices or officers, ethics audits, and institutional policy statements (such as guidelines for "Do not resuscitate" orders or affirmative action in hiring). The inside source of the norms and sanctions may make them both more compelling and more appropriate because they emerge from knowledge of the immediate context and its peculiar problems. On the other hand, codes and committees may be mere public-relations exhibits or guardians of moral minimums rather than expressions of pervasive concerns in the institution. They may focus narrowly on certain behaviors rather than on larger concerns such as commitment to shared values. Their sanctions may be toothless, and they may lack any critical measures of moral responsibility beyond the welfare of the institution as conceived at the top.

What the fence approach neglects above all is the quality of life in the corral. Fences set limits, but they set only a fraction of the tone. Inside the fences, morality is more an ethos than a set of constraining circles. Whatever values really drive the operation are part of the air that institutional participants breathe. The culture of the institution imparts and implies standards of acceptability and approval. Recruitment and training of employees, models of leadership, development and revision of statements of purpose, networks of communication, styles of decision making, criteria for evaluation, and examples of good community citizenship give an identity to the institution and its members as part of it. Moving beyond letter to spirit and beyond designated ethical considerations to a whole style of working together and relating to the various constituencies and publics the institution touches, a cultural focus attends as much to stories, images, heroines, and heroes as to standards and prohibitions. The assets of this approach include its recognition of the presence and importance of values in every phase of the institution's life and its move beyond minimal stipulations to maximal embodiment.

This cultural emphasis trips alarm signals when participants in the culture of the institution become, either by drift or by design, totally institutionalized. Loyalty to the institution, in those instances, allows no room for higher loyalties or competing loyalties. No leeway then remains for institutional self-criticism or recognition of transcendent norms. A simple cultural approach offers no way of judging one culture better than another except to measure its influential power. What morality should be elevated remains an open question.

Societal regulation, institutional formal restraints, and institutional culture are all critically important. Institutional ethical health will normally require all three. Social restraints assure a level of responsibility that denies an institution the license of being left to its own devices. Formal internal restraints keep ethical issues in view as part of the institution's own commitments. The institutional ethos or culture constitutes the acid test of what values actually govern the life of the institution beyond the dictates of law and the vigilence of internal monitoring. When the three layers function effectively, they can provide both mutual reinforcement and mutual correction, but keeping all three layers in place does not guarantee that the values they reinforce or the direction of the correction will be all that is desired. How does one judge the moral responsibility of an institution other than by the consistency of its commitments with societal regulation and internal code?

Stages of Institutional Moral Development

The fence approach aims at assuring an acceptable level of institutional responsibility by regulating actions, but it does not deal adequately with institutional character. A ladder approach offers better possibilities for evaluating the level of responsibility in an institution's culture. If we were discussing the moral responsibility of individuals, we would need to consider such influential theories of moral development as those of Lawrence Kohlberg and Carol Gilligan.[3] Since institutions are the objects of our reflection, we might assume that the stages delineated by these theorists are irrelevant. But are they? If institutions are, in some ways, moral agents, as was claimed in the previous chapter, it might be thinkable to evaluate their moral maturity by appropriating the findings and rankings of these two psychologists. And, since personal moral development is inseparable from the influences of social settings, there might be useful parallels to explore.

We can posit at the outset that, due to their complexity and population size, institutions will usually function at several stages simultaneously. Parts of institutions may exemplify a particular stage more than others, just as individuals in the institution will. And we can assume that institutions, like individuals, do not completely leave all reversion to lower stages behind in moving to higher stages.

Kohlberg delineates three levels of moral development (preconventional, conventional, and postconventional or principled) and breaks each level down into two stages. At his preconventional level, people are moved by a desire to avoid punishment and a recognition of the superior power of another at the first stage and by a desire to gain personal benefit through advantageous trade-offs at the second stage. Fear of apprehension and punishment keeps people straight at the lowest stage and preserving the perks of an arrangement dictates behavior at the next one.

In institutional development we could call the preconventional level the *constraint* level and divide it between a *coercive* stage and a *contractual* stage. At the first, an institution's moral practice is a function of the fear of sanctions for breach of either societal laws or institutional codes; at the second, the various parties in the institutional mix continue to cooperate solely because of the advantages afforded by the continued affiliation. At stage one we all know we had better keep our noses clean or risk bad consequences; at stage two we keep our part of the bargain if we expect others to do so and thus benefit us through our joint involvement in the institution.

To Kohlberg's conventional level, we can parallel an institutional *cultural* level. His stage three, conformity to mutual interpersonal expectations and relationships, can simply be expanded to mean *conformity* to a corporate culture that defines the good employee, the good manager, the good marketer, the good nurse, the good caseworker, or the good professor. The institution makes its expectations clear, and people want to please. The institution is now the significant other whose approval the loyal member craves.

In Kohlberg's fourth stage, a person is committed to the maintenance of the system and resistant to disordering exception taking in deference to the authority that represents the system. The institutional parallel is the organization, where loyalty to the institution has been thoroughly ingrained. Valuing what the institution stands for pervades the culture, and thus everyone is inclined to *consent* to institutional authority, however expressed. Boss knows best. Disorder is destructive. The system sustains.

What then would correspond to Kohlberg's postconventional and principled level with its stages five and six? At stage five one sees the greater benefits of entering a social contract and abiding by the will of the majority. One allows the socially contracted norms to over-rule personal or group desires because of the goodness of the process that produced them. One is committed to the democratic process because it produces the greatest good for the greatest number. When the group decides an issue fairly, one should support the decision so long as basic human rights are not violated.

At the sixth stage, one feels obligated to treat others fairly and justly because one subscribes to universal moral principles. Allegiance to what Kohlberg sees as universal norms makes a "rational" person willing to cross convention and resist conformity.

As institutional parallels, we might designate the postconventional level as the level of *conscientious community* and delineate stages of *consensus* (five) and *conscience* (six). In both instances, the way is opened for narrow institutional self-interest to be transcended. Stage five asks who is heard and considered in the institution's inner dialogue or conscience. If the process of decision making is inclusive, then the participants can accept the decisions as ways to secure the greatest good for the greatest number. Stage six elevates the shared values that provide the glue for the community, the values that Selznick calls the "vehicles of group identity"; these values stretch beyond mere institutional reinforcement to institutional self-criticism. In the case of stage five, the democratic participation that accompanies decision making protects rights and interests that might otherwise be neglected; at stage six, the voice of dissent and criticism is incorporated into the institution's "information net," as Stone dubs it,[4] and its structures of decision making. In keeping with A. L. Schorr's urging, sedition is built in;[5] criticism is encouraged. The fifth stage focuses on the hearing aids in the institution's structure that assure voice to all affected people. The sixth affirms norms that should govern institutional life even if a majority might be inclined to ignore them.

Using women subjects, Carol Gilligan has uncovered numerous weaknesses in Kohlberg's predominantly male-based research. His autonomous individuals applying abstract moral principles are exchanged for contextual selves in webs of relationships attempting to respond to the needs and interests of all the people involved. In calling this highest level of institutional moral development communal, I am leaning more toward Gilligan's relational model than toward Kohlberg's rational model, more toward a relational conscience than a conscience equipped with universal rational principles. Kohlberg's scale peaks at an abstract principle of justice, Gilligan's at a relational web of caring.

Gilligan's stage one, which is driven by care for individual survival, would have its institutional parallel in an organizational ethos with the reigning assumption that all performance appeals must be pitched at the level of avoiding bad consequences either directly to the individual or to the institution, with personal losses following in the wake. The institution's only aim would be to guarantee its survival.

Her stage two defines goodness in terms of caring for others to the exclusion of care for one's self. The institutional parallel here might be either an institutional ethos that demands total submersion of personal needs and rights for the sake of the institution or an institutional willingness to sacrifice itself for some larger social good. Institutions in general resist their own demise, at either their own initiative or that of others. The business corporation thus finds itself caught in an awkward contradiction. It is bent on assuring its own survival, yet it also gives its allegiance to an economic system that claims that some corporations should die for the good of the system. In theory no one is too good to go if foreign competition bests you or your buggy is superseded by another's car. In practice the company is apt to lobby for protective legislation, bailouts, and other forms of governmental assistance to survival.

For the individual, Gilligan effectively disparages the equation of self-obliteration with exemplary morality, and no institution should ask a person, in the words of one traditional marriage service, to forsake all others and cleave only unto it. Correspondingly, expecting self-obliteration by an institution for the sake of another institution or of some higher cause is asking too much under normal circumstances. Just as employees can learn to accept retirement, feeling that they have completed an appropriate term of service and knowing that some turnover in personnel is healthy for the institution, an institution that has served its purpose might well phase itself out gracefully. There is, however, no Social Security check or retirement plan for institutions. Institutions should no more be expected to commit suicide than individuals should be expected to resign voluntarily to help out the organization when they have no other source of livelihood in sight.

Gilligan's final stage or level three elevates interdependence. It affirms moral equality between self and others and advocates a caring that attends to the needs and value of both. The institutional equivalent would entail recognition by the policies, practices, and personnel in the organization of an obligation to care not only about the institution's well-being but also about the other personal or group interests present in the institution, about the well-being of other related institutions, and about the larger public good. Transcendence of narrow institutional self-interest would grow out of seeing the coincidence of the institution's long-term interests with those of the larger society and, at best, even of the global community. You may be wondering whether a bureaucratic organization can become a network of care, and we may be talking about rare birds. Another problem with Gilligan's top level is that conscience and community may find their integrity around questionable centers of loyalty and that interdependence may be narrowly conceived. Nationalism, for instance, is vulnerable to criticism on both counts.

Both Kohlberg and Gilligan provide useful measures for institutional as well as individual moral maturity, but Kohlberg would probably not expect rational self-transcendence by institutions, and, by definition, Gilligan's project does not address the reasons why an institution's sense of interdependence should have global reach. We are still left with the question of what normative measures should be used to evaluate and reform institutional cultures.

Sources of Ethical Guidance

In seeking norms for institutional responsibility, we have to ask what sources for such norms institutions can be expected to acknowledge. Religious traditions offer norms, but how can these be accepted in the pluralistic institutions of an even more pluralistic society in an even more pluralistic world? Of course, religious institutions, such as churches, have a mandate to follow a particular ethic, whether they do so or not. Furthermore, wherever persons with strong commitments to the moral guidance of a particular religious tradition hold sway over an institution, they can insist on considerable conformity to their ethical standards at the overt behavioral level, provided they do not infringe on people's legal rights. Still further, our secular institutions may continue to reflect the religious influences in our culture, even amid protestations to the contrary. But assuming that most institutions do not have the religious definition that many ecclesiastical organizations inherit or adopt, and that the leadership of most institutions will find it either distasteful or ineffectual to promulgate an ethic in the institution because "the Bible tells us so" or "my religion dictates it so," to what authority can we appeal other than the law of the land or the favor of the consumer or the wrath of ownership?

Recourse to human "rationality" and some universally acknowledged morality offers limited help for several reasons. The first is the elusiveness of the content of this morality that all rational beings supposedly know and espouse. What seems perfectly rational to most people in Iran or China may not always seem so to most people in the United States. We have lived such different stories that we often make sense of things differently. Even within our own country, it becomes more and more questionable to assume immersion in a common story. The vaunted voice of reason is heard differently by people from different backgrounds with different makeups functioning in different institutional settings. Even members of the same family with similar histories and outlooks have been heard to scream that other members are being irrational because they do not see particular problems or situations the way the screamers do. Our self-interest slants our reasoning. We reason out of commitments and in contexts. Similarities of human experience teach shared distaste for dehumanizing conditions and enable communication about freedom and justice between cultures, but anyone familiar with the difficulty of communicating ideas in a different language will appreciate the barriers to uniform, universal understanding of ethical principles.

Even when people agree on certain moral principles, that agreement assures neither general agreement on their applicability in particular circumstances nor general willingness to do what is acknowledged to be right. Charles McCoy observes that business executives and social activists sometimes come from similar religious backgrounds and share certain values yet interpret their value commitments in different institutional locations and conflict with each other about the implications of those cherished values.[6] Freedom and justice not only may mean different things to different people; they may take on different meaning in different settings for the same people. They also receive only lip service when personal or institutional gain is at stake.

People must share more than intellectual capacity if they are to share moral values, and they must share more than common institutional membership if those values are to be more than instruments for the reinforcement of institutional self-interest narrowly conceived. What shares, what common stocks, what common stories might afford bases for institutional ethics in our society? Family life was long trusted to teach common lessons about covenantal relatedness, but the decline of the traditional family and the great diversity in what people either have learned from it or have substituted for it often make family stories more divisive than convergent. A globally shared story may be an emerging possibility in a shrinking world with a shared stake in ozone layers, arable soil, potable water, and reduction of nuclear weapons, but its gestation is just moving beyond being a gleam in ecologists' and conservationists' eyes. While we wait for that story to unfold, there are three existing shared stories that are potential moral guides—those of nation, profession, and corporation.

As U.S. citizens, we share more than the authority of certain laws and governmental officials. We supposedly have mutual commitments to democratic values. The laws cannot capture all we hold dear in the Constitution and the Bill of Rights. Call it America's "civil religion" with Robert Bellah[7] or "self-evident truths" with the

Founding Fathers, we depend in our common life on our being shareholders in a moral legacy. All three branches of government are engaged in the endless task of spelling out new ramifications of that legacy for each new day.

As partners in professions or occupations, we share common stories and hold common stocks. To be a teacher or an engineer, a doctor or a nurse, a journalist or an architect, a lawyer or a business manager, a minister or a social worker, is to join a history and to acquire stock in the stature and aims of a particular vocation. The image of our vocation carries moral freight and moral expectations. Role models precede and surround us. Standards judge us. Past failings in our profession may spur us. Ideals beckon us.

As employees of hospitals, nursing homes, businesses, schools, firms, and agencies, we also enter a history—of a particular hospital and of all hospitals, of our corporation and of others, of our school and, to some degree, of every school. We probably operate with some shared assumptions about why the institution exists, what its purposes are, and what allegiance it demands. Whether in the form of a previous reputation to live down or a new societal challenge to meet or some well-defined institutional code of ethics, our institutional placement has moral meaning.

From any or all of these potential common shares or sources, can we derive any bases for institutional moral responsibility? Although the idea is tightly linked to the Jewish and Christian religious traditions, there is also justification for making the covenantal relationship such a basis on the other grounds we have cited.

As Robert Bellah spells out in *The Broken Covenant*, two Americas have coexisted in uneasy tension since the time of our nation's origins—the covenantal community of John Winthrop and contractual "coagulation of individual interests" described by Thomas Hobbes and John Locke.[8] Early New Englanders affirmed not only an inner covenant between believers and God but an outward, national covenant that obligated all citizens to each other as well as to God. This biblical idea and the Roman legacy of a democratic republic dependent on people's willingness to act in the interest of the larger community were countered early by the drive for individual success and the belief that pursuit of private gain by each would produce the public good for all. That tension has at times made for a delicate balance in our national story, but we have lately witnessed the breach of the covenant and the demise of zeal for the public good.

Despite this sorry state, which Bellah bemoaned first in *The Broken Covenant* and more recently in *Habits of the Heart*, the American experience still carries evidences of our origins and memories of our finest hours. Suspicion of concentrated power, belief that laws and the values they embody are more important than the people in power, and concern for those in need still rouse at such moments as the Watergate hearings and concerted campaigns for the hungry and homeless. Persistent appeals for broader participation in institutional decision making also reflect the continuing dynamism of democratic values. Our sense of covenantal obligation to each other is like a language we once knew but use now with difficulty, to employ the metaphor that the authors of *Habits of the Heart* often suggest, but it is not yet an unknown tongue for many if not most Americans.

Covenantal understandings of professions and of the institutions in which they work also surface on close examination. In *The Physician's Covenant*, William F. May emphasizes the crucial importance of the distinction between covenants and contracts for doctors. Covenants, unlike contracts, are rooted in gifts that imply obligations, and these gifts point ultimately to a religious basis of covenantal commitment. Traditionally, physicians practiced with a sense of gratitude for what they owed to their forerunners in the profession and in scientific discovery, to their own teachers, to their patients, to their communities, and ultimately to a divine giver—understood in either Hippocratic or biblical fashion. They were part of a sacred covenant. May believes that this covenantal model has largely lost out to philanthropic and contractual ones: optional giving to those in need and selling services to those who require them.

In his challenge to create "covenanted institutions" that can counteract the liabilities of bureaucratic hierarchy, narrow specialization, and impersonal treatment, May at times seems to say that covenantal institutions are only possible for those who have covenantal religious commitments, but he cracks the door to greater inclusiveness: "Institutions, consciously or unconsciously, embody a covenant, a social purpose, a human good, which they avow and serve. And in the course of rendering that service, institutions receive as well as give to the community."[9] Institutions then have or should have covenantal reasons for existing. In health care, contractual understandings of professional or institutional relations to the patient and the community tend to narrow obligations to short-term treatment of the diseases that patients present instead of long-term concern for the health of needy persons and communities that covenants entail.

Traditionally Western corporations have had a particular history that distinguishes them from many corporations in the East and in many developing countries where old family networks are linked to the group in control of the government. Following the patterns of first the medieval church and then the medieval city as institutional centers independent of the household and the political regime, Protestant lawyers formed limited-liability corporations in the seventeenth century (first designated joint-stock companies) for commercial purposes. Emerging as the first glimmers of political democracy were also appearing, these arrangements allowed people to invest without risking more than their investment.

In sketching this history, Max Stackhouse suggests that the ethos that enabled these corporations to develop and pervaded their operations still influences people working in corporations, whether they acknowledge or appreciate their tradition or not. "Common economic action demands a work ethic, a set of values separate from familial and political control, a discipline guided by rational control, at least a sense of 'profession,' and a stewardship of wealth that is not one's own."[10] Early religious roots of this ethos have largely been forgotten by a contractual and utilitarian society, but some of the heritage persists in the culture of corporate life. This heritage is not contractual; nor is it patriarchal (ascribing divine right to the top bananas in the hierarchy); it is covenantal. It sets institutional life in the context of a structure of accountability that assumes that the corporation has a separate and even sacred vocation.

McCoy contends that corporations are no exception to the rule that social organizations are covenantal, whether the commitments are explicitly spelled out or not. As he expresses it, "Like all other social groups, corporations are based upon covenants that define the patterns of interaction and limitations."[11] Corporate charters issued by state governments are one evidence of a covenant between a corporation and society, but McCoy also points to covenants in the surrounding society that set terms for corporate life. Common purposes and values in the society, expressed in laws, in resource allocations, and in implicit or explicit moral directives, reveal this covenantal context of the corporation. This context is the key for understanding what such principles as freedom and justice mean in corporate life.

Although McCoy is a theologian, he derives the criteria he uses to develop "a comprehensive ethic for corporate policy" from what corporate managers say about (1) corporate self-interest, (2) multiple responsibility, and (3) social vision.[12] For each of these criteria, expansion is the route to greater ethical responsibility in a corporation—expansion of the meaning of corporate self-interest to include societal interest, expansion of the multiple responsibilities to all stakeholders in corporate activities, and expansion of social vision to include broader and more distant horizons as well as overlooked needs close at hand. Corporate self-interest is not institutional sin if it grasps the inseparability and interdependence of corporate interest and larger community interest. There is a vast difference between assuming that whatever is good for my company is bound to be good for the society and recognizing that the long-term good of the society is essential to the long-term good of the company. Multiple responsibility should include all affected constituencies touched by the life and product of the corporation. Social vision should see beyond the immediate to the long-term future and the larger social good. Each of these expansions makes sense in a covenantal context rather than a contractual one.

McCoy also examines the implications of each of three sets of American social values for the life of a firm. The Smithian (as in Adam Smith) value system stresses pursuit of self-interest and productivity. The humanitarian value system elevates respect for individual rights and provision of equal opportunity. The communitarian value system, which carries on the covenantal tradition, emphasizes community membership and the good of the whole. All three value systems command significant commitment in our society, but, when he wrote *Management of Values*, McCoy believed that the growing strength of communitarian values would bring expanded versions of corporate self-interest, multiple responsibility, and social vision. The recent political mood of the country and recent diagnoses of our nation's radical individualism in such places as *Habits of the Heart* would deny that the forces at work toward communitarian values are as strong as such covenantal advocates as McCoy have hoped; still, talk about a Japanese management style and the emphasis on nurture of loyalty in corporate cultures has supported a more communitarian and covenantal idea of business institutions than our individualism would supposedly espouse.

We can also discover covenantal understandings of professions and institutions in places where the word *covenant* is not used. In advocating "being faithful" and four other moral principles (respecting autonomy, avoiding harm, benefiting others, and being just) as a guide for student-affairs professionals in higher education, Karen Strohm Kitchener does not claim that these principles are self-evident to any rational person. Rather, they are "both necessary to and implicit in the ethical practice of student services work." She writes, "Even if all people are not bound by the principle of being faithful, those in the helping professions acquire a special obligation to be so by virtue of the roles ascribed to them: that is, to help, to be deemed trustworthy."[13] She posits an implicit "contract" or agreement that underlies the work of a human-services professional, and she considers the concept of contract central to the university's obligation as an institution. This sense of an underlying structure of fidelity is critical, but *covenant* provides a richer image for that implicit agreement than contract. Moreover, the proximity of *vocation* to *covenant* is apparent in Kitchener's reference to a "special obligation" residing in certain roles.

In the same volume, LuAnn Krager's application of being faithful to the roles of the student-services professional also points beyond contract, with its minimal and temporary implications, to covenant, although that word is never used. "Fidelity," she states, "can be measured in behavior over time and also in consistency of word and deed." Her exposition speaks of the "time and trust" required "to establish relationships that support effective communication and that help new ideas to evolve into workable plans" of honoring commitments and of promise keeping.[14] This covenantal language stretches the context of fidelity beyond mere contracts and defines student-services professionals as socially located members rather than as "rational" agents appropriating abstract principles. These professionals stand in the tradition of helping professions, and their obligations should concern them with persons in their wholeness, not with students as mere consumers of services.

Writing about social work, Robert Pruger warns professionals working in the bureaucratic environments of social agencies that they must learn to be good bureaucrats despite the fact that their training has not taught them how. They must learn to meet institutional expectations, to understand institutional authority and organization, and to acquire the requisite skills to command respect and function effectively in that setting. Nevertheless, Pruger urges "the good bureaucrat" to be "a vital presence," to develop staying power, and to keep pushing to enlarge the zone of discretion in one's position. He warns that a "special kind of commitment or strength is required to maintain an independence of mind" when the helper feels a strong identification with the organization.[15] The character or virtue that he advocates assures that institutional acculturation of its members will never be complete, no matter how noble the institution's purposes, and thereby assures institutional health. The social worker must, he insists, serve the mission of the helping organization, not the organization itself. Although he does not use the words, Pruger implies that both the social worker and the helping organization have special social obligations that we would call covenantal and vocational. If we are to label the virtues he promotes, we might call his staying power patience, his ability to exercise independent judgment wisdom and courage, and his refusal to take the institution too seriously a sense of humor. He is silent on the virtues of covenantal institutions.

Measuring Institutional Responsibility

In our search for moral measures of institutional and professional responsibility that go beyond institutional self-interest and personal self-interest, we have appropriated the assistance offered by the fences of regulatory limitation and the ladders of developmental maturity without discovering which norms or values should be used in our assessments of secular institutions and professional obligations. In our effort to find bases for these measures which are not the sole possession of one religious tradition, yet which do not presume some universal content shared by all rational people, we have explored the covenantal contexts assumed by some renditions of the stories of our nation, our professions, and our institutions. In that covenantal context, rooted and reinforced in our biblical religious traditions but not confined to them, what guidance for institutions emerges in terms of (1) ends and consequences, (2) obligations and rights, and (3) virtues and character?

Central to any concern for institutional responsibility is the question of the harmony or disharmony between the ends our institutions claim and the ends they actually serve. Institutions tend to become ends in themselves and not to serve their purposes. As William F. May says of hospitals, we must keep reminding ourselves that their reason for being is provision of health care, and that should include prevention as well as treatment of illness. Institutions are obliged, if they are to gain and keep public support and internal loyalty, to keep holding their professed ends up against their actual practice and their promised outcomes up against their actual effects.

Max Stackhouse makes it a matter of institutional vocation: "If a university becomes a political party or a psychiatric center, if a corporation becomes a military camp or a charity organization, if a church becomes a museum or a court of law, it has betrayed its central vocation." Totalitarian regimes, he reminds us, tend to turn education into propaganda, industry into military supply, law into politics, art into ideology, and religion into either a means of repression or a focus of persecution.[16]

Michael Smith calls this distinctive institutional reason for being its "idiosyncratic purpose." For him, the "virtue" of such an institution as a hospital is measured by its very nature and mission. If the institution has built-in structures and relationships, such as peer evaluation and required continuing education that enable it to perform its purpose with more regularity and greater ease, it is a virtuous agent. It has the institutional equivalent of good habits, as understood by Aristotle and Thomas Aquinas. Such virtue, according to Smith, goes beyond what a contract can require.[17] We would call it covenantal.

Institutions can and should be held responsible for violating the public trust, an implicit or explicit covenant that grants them life as contributors to the public good. If, for instance, a corporation is providing not goods and services, but "bads" and "disservices" to society, it has betrayed that trust and forfeited the right to exist. If colleges not only fail to enlighten the young but actually corrupt them (a matter of interpretation, we must admit, especially in light of the charge against Socrates that he corrupted the young), they will lose public confidence and support. If hospitals not only do not make us better or handle us with care but make bad matters worse by prolonging death, increasing suffering, or making us sicker with the treatment than we were with the disease, they will trigger public protest and rejection. We should evaluate institutions, at least in part, on the basis of the values they exalt and on the basis of what they, in fact, do in light of what they profess to do for the society that gives them life. To what kind of futures are they leading for the next generations? What restrictions and regulations do they require to assure that their protestations about contributions to the common good come true? What effects on the ecosystem do they cause?

In order to gain and hold public support, institutions must at least appear to serve some social or environmental good, and the values they exalt can become the measures of their acceptability. Even more important, every human good must be watched lest it be taken with ultimate seriousness and thus deified. What H. Richard Niebuhr called "radical monotheism"[18] means, for institutions, not that they are expected to become worshipers of the God above all human idols, but that we should build critical safeguards into each institution to protect its members against idolizing the institution's ends or the institution itself. For instance, even if we are working to make people healthier, we may end up trampling autonomy or forgetting other human goods.

What of obligations, principles, rules, and rights, which institutions should be expected to observe? Procedures, codes of conduct, statements by administrative officials, policies of institutions, and the means of their enforcement testify to an institution's commitment to such obligations as protection of rights of privacy for patients, clients, and employees and elimination of conflicts of interest. Limits on irresponsibility and mandates for responsibility are spelled out in such statements as those dealing with withdrawal of treatment in intensive-care units or hiring practices or standards of evaluation, promotion, and censure. What normative expectations should underlie the duties and prohibitions an institution promulgates?

A covenantal conception of institutions implies at least three mandates. These are obligations to inclusiveness, to treatment with attentive respect, and to empowerment. Inclusiveness takes account of the well-being of all the persons and constituencies that are touched, or should be touched, by the institution's presence and activity. Treatment with respect encompasses the needs of the whole person, not just the physical or material needs, and not just the social or psychological needs. To respect people is to deal with them as persons, not just as patients, clients, customers, or employees. Empowerment seeks the fullest possible exercise of people's human potentialities within the constraints of institutional limits. It means giving people voice, decision-making participation, and responsibility. It means nurturing the growth of people whose lives the institution affects. In sum, covenantal commitments oblige us to extend care both extensively and intensively.[19]

The obligation to respect and care for people and for our natural environment as well is supported not only by much philosophical and religious thought about ethics, but also by many institutional statements of mission and policy. More than that, it is supported by the experience of alienation felt by people in relation to institutions that violate or ignore human dignity. The critical issues become those of depth and scope—the depth of concern for each person, including a concern for a person's empowerment, and the reach of concern beyond the boundaries we are always erecting.

Institutions often manifest a momentum toward circumscription in defining their community or communities of concern, in defining the slice of an individual's life that makes a claim on institutional attention, and in defining a person's sphere or scope of responsibility within the institution. Faced with a deluge of clients and potential clients and a drought of resources, social agencies, for instance, many standardize clients by stereotyping, by screening to reduce the pool of potential claimants for attention, and by isolating a small slice of what is often a much larger and more complex problem. People needing help then are more likely to fall between the institutional cracks and to be defeated by the bureaucratic runaround they perceive in their treatment. The whole person in a web of relationships and a problem-ridden environment gets lost in the shuffle of paper and feet.

H. Richard Niebuhr, on the other hand, perceived a self-transcending impetus in human societies. As he explains in *The Responsible Self*, human societies point beyond themselves toward causes, ideals, values, or founders for which the group stands. These higher purposes or centers of group life are significant reasons for people's allegiance to a community or institution. People are bound together in relation to some third. The higher the reach of this third, the broader usually will be the inclusiveness of the community encompassed by loyalty to it. For Niebuhr the theologian, the vicissitudes of life are continually revealing the clay feet of our little gods and turning us toward a faith in the God above all human idols who will place us in a universal community with all of being: "The societies that judge or in which we judge ourselves are self-transcending societies. And the process of self-transcendence or reference to the third beyond each third does not come to rest until the total community of being has been involved."[20] We cannot ask institutions to profess Niebuhr's faith, but for him democracy leads toward affirmation of universal society just as monotheism does.

Corporations, universities, social agencies, and medical centers are usually not fully democratic, although the best ones seek greater participation in management. Neither are they communities "lived in praise of God," to borrow from T. S. Eliot ("Choruses from 'the Rock'"). However, self-transcending proclivities do keep showing up. Robert Brown contends that the sense of community in an institution of higher education should stretch to the whole of higher education as a community, to the nation as a community, and even to the earth as a community.[21] The companies surveyed by the Business Roundtable do recognize expanding multiple responsibilities. For instance, the credo of Johnson and Johnson states, "We are responsible to the communities in which we live and work and to the world community as well." Although Dow Chemical Company is not in the group covered by the survey, its objectives include the following: "To seek maximum long-term profit growth as the primary means to insure the prosperity of our employees and stockholders, the well-being of our customers, and the improvement of people's lives everywhere. . . . To practice stewardship of the manufacture, marketing, use and disposal of our products. To share in the responsibility of all peoples for protection of the environment. To make wise and efficient use of the earth's energy and natural resources. To make this world a better place for our having been in business."[22] Some of us remember the protests against Dow because of what the napalm it manufactured during the Vietnam War did to people, including many innocent children and adult civilians, but this statement still illustrates our point.

Institutional codes at their best push the application of such principles as avoiding harm, providing benefit, respecting autonomy, and doing justice to broader rather than narrower constituencies and stakeholders. Codes of professions at their best stretch the accountability and reach of their members' obligations as they function in corporations, medical centers, schools, and other institutions.

The interests of the least powerful, least advantaged, and most needy are usually ignored or neglected by institutions that are not directly answerable to those constituencies. Although announced institutional moral principles often push toward inclusion, their implementation will generally stop well short of fully embracing universal community. Steps toward inclusiveness include practicing nondiscrimination concerning sex, race, or age; acknowledging some level of environmental responsibility; and obeying government as the supposed representative of the larger society. Beyond mere nondiscrimination, various forms of affirmative action attack the problems of institutional racism and sexism by extra efforts to change the mix of decison-makers and policy-setters, as well as to expand the opportunities of those in groups that have been deprived of them.

These measures change institutional cultures by their inclusiveness and get at structural problems that often are more the residue of past societal subordinations and discriminations than the result of current intentions in the institution. Such institutional policies are important initiatives toward institutional inclusiveness, although they do not exhaust the obligation to be inclusive. Responsible institutions are obligated to find ways to give voice to those who are touched by the work of the institution or who look to the institution for care or empowerment, especially those people who are most vulnerable and powerless.

The way communication flows into and out of an institution, the way it flows up and down within an institution, and the way power is shared give evidence of degrees of inclusiveness, attentiveness, and empowerment. Pushing toward greater inclusiveness of all affected and realistically affectable persons, respectful attentiveness to the needs of the total person, and further empowerment of all those with the capacity to decide and act on matters affecting them are the institutional equivalents of love and justice, but love is ultimately more a quality of personal and corporate life than a principle of institutional governance. And justice relies on a spirit of fairness, not just a system of protections. Care is not captured by codes, nor is it infused by them. It takes a total institutional culture to embody and nurture such virtues or qualities. But can institutions have virtues other than what Michael Smith described as organization habits that facilitate the service of their purposes?

There is abundant testimony to the importance of trust, patience, honesty, fidelity, integrity, and compassion among the employees of an institution. Pruger, for example, reminds us that "the qualities and capabilities of people," not just the structure of the organization, are part of the equation in a bureaucracy.[23] We can also find descriptions of qualities that are requisite for exemplary moral leadership from institutional executives and other leaders. In *Creating Excellence*, Craig Hickman and Michael Silva extol an impressive list of virtues as crucial executive assets for managing corporate culture, strategy, and change. These are creative insight, sensitivity, vision, versatility, focus, and patience.[24] The authors promote the virtues as means of managerial success, but several of the companies briefed in *Corporate Ethics* illustrate the presence and influence of ethically responsible corporate leaders who exemplify virtues that are not merely instrumental to institutional success.

What is more, writing on institutional cultures in that selective survey and elsewhere recognizes that the truly ethical company is the one in which its credo, as it is said of Johnson and Johnson's credo, "has crept into everyone's value system"; it has become "the unifying force of the corporation." Interestingly enough, their credo is called "a living document," "an employee's document," and "a set of relationships," not a set of rules. Earlier we also noted GTE's philosophy, which holds that "the organization as a whole needs to provide the environment and mechanisms for supporting ethical practice."[25]

What virtues, then, can we ask of an institution's culture—that is, its patterns of decision making, its stories about itself, its networks of communication, and its personnel policies? Michael Smith makes covenantal virtue possible for an institution in the sense of structured, habitual pursuit of its purpose, but the content of such virtue comes down to efficiency in the accomplishment of its ends. The only other virtue he treats is prudence or practical wisdom. For a hospital, for instance, that virtue would direct that hiring, teamwork, in-service training policies, and peer review should "facilitate the regular use of relevant information."[26] The virtue of prudence differs from virtue in pursuit of an institution's distinctive purpose because it is a virtue for any person and thus for any institution; its excellence is not tied to a particular aim or end of the institution. A law firm and a hospital serve different ends, but both should build prudence into their operations. Can there also be institutional equivalents of trust, fidelity, honesty, humility, self-denial, patience, and compassion? Can institutions be covenantal, not just contractual, by embodying these qualities? Here comes that very claim.

Policies, structures, processes, recognitions, and mission statements can set a mood or tone, can nurture attitudes and concerns, and can embody priorities and values. The continual refrain about trust and concern for employees in the language and literature of Hewlett-Packard is borne out in management style, company strategy, and corporate decision making. Ethics is seldom mentioned as a separate topic, but trust is reflected in assurance of job security, in the prevailing assumption that people want to do a good job, in the absence of time clocks, and in the avoidance of close monitoring and punitive measures. "Belief in people" is the working premise.[27] This belief, which cannot be captured or engendered by a code alone, expresses institutional trust and nurtures a community of trust. In a time when general polygraph testing and drug testing of employees have been hotly argued issues, the contrast is striking.

Institutional patience is reflected in willingness to look at long-term rather than short-term results in evaluating personal and institutional accomplishments, in the lengths to which an institution goes to discover why an employee has "peaked out" or "burned out" and what can be done to salvage the person. One might call this stance "hope" as well. Patience is also revealed in the time an employee can safely devote to getting to the bottom of clients' or patients' or customers' real concerns, or, better, in company recognition of such attentiveness by employees to those served.

Institutional humility is embodied where hierarchical tendencies are counteracted by programs and processes that decentralize power and authority. Management with consultation rather than by edict, open communication, respect for subordinates, team cooperation, built-in checks and balances, and democratic participation in decisions are all manifestations of institutional humility, the concerted effort to avoid taking the institution too seriously. GTE's Employee Survey Program, for instance, actively seeks information about the perceived health of the corporation from the entire work force "without flinching from the bad news that is inevitable" in such polling.[28] As Schorr urges, institutions can build sedition into the bureaucracy. Institutional structure and policy can make the equivalent of the Socratic gadfly not only permitted but expected and even mandated.

Institutional self-denial is evident in the recognition that one institution should not define a person's total life and cannot define the public good. The policies and culture of an institution can assert that a person is more than the roles he or she plays in the life of that institution. Parental leaves, in-house day-care facilities, and protection of an employee's right to follow personal convictions publicly through involvement in political causes and social action exemplify institutional self-denial.

What McCoy calls "social vision" is also a virtue that can be embodied institutionally. The perspicacity of institutional research and planning will depend on how broadly an organization's planners scan the societal environment of the organization and how deeply they probe in discerning and anticipating societal problems on which its institutional life does impinge or could impinge. The keenness of the institution's eyesight will depend on the amount of staff time, the mix of people, and the financial resources it is willing to devote to its review of its social setting and its future strategic alternatives. For instance, how, why, and by whom was the decision made to develop the next new wing of the medical center for obstetrics or neonatology instead of gerontology?

Fidelity and compassion are manifest in long-term commitment to employees and clients. For instance, the provisions an institution makes to assist a peaked-out employee, an alcoholic employee, or an employee whose job disappears during a recession reveal the pres-

ence or absence of fidelity and care in the institution, not just in one
or two individuals within it. Follow-up services for patients and families by hospitals and other health agencies are also forms of institutional fidelity defining commitment to people as continuing and not
episodic. Such care also encompasses the total needs of the person
and does not focus narrowly on a disease or isolated aspect of what
may be a constellation of problems in a family or other set of relationships. Providing staffs for intensive-care units that include social
workers, psychiatrists, chaplains, and ethicists is a form of institutional fidelity and care.

"Patient" care for people with urinary incontinence affords a
striking illustration of the need to make their care an institutional
concern as well as the personal concern of certain members of the
staff. The great temptation of the rushed professional is to assume
that the incontinent patient will remain that way and to equate care
with inserting and checking catheters and changing diapers, underpads, and bed linen. The current reimbursement system encourages such an attitude. Institutions get reimbursed for catheters,
catheter bags, gloves, diapers, and underpads, not for hours spent
reeducating patients. The more demanding approach sees incontinence as a symptom, attempts to discover and deal with the underlying causes where that is possible, and helps the patient change
through environmental modification, retraining, and treatment.[29]
This approach takes time—time to take patient histories, time to
have consultations with a variety of health-care colleagues, and time
to work with the patient to bring change. It also takes support from
colleagues on the staff and support from the administration of the
hospital or nursing home to allow a nurse or other staff member the
time to deal with the problem at a deeper level. Care, then, needs to
be an institutional virtue, not just a personal one.

A certain public health clinic for children was the site of this
memorable vignette of institutional patience and care. To allay a
child's fears of being examined, a nurse practitioner carried out a
full examination on the boy's teddy bear. The whole staff was willing
to take time, not only in this instance but as a general practice, to
explain things to parents. Mothers who took their children there did
not feel rushed or patronized. They felt that the staff, nearly all of
them women, believed in their ability to handle their responsibilities and to learn what they needed to know.[30] That sounds like trust
on top of patience and care.

Care of high quality depends not only on the virtue of a particular
institution, but also on the virtue built into a system of linkages
between institutions. For instance, patients who can leave the hospital but still need technological support may face lack of services and

linkages in their communities. In response to this problem, France and England, for example, have developed regional systems of coordinated care for technology-dependent people. Chronic ventilator patients are even able to remain in their communities. Some of the features of the system include group purchase of medical supplies, equipment repair, and patient education.[31]

The 1988–89 findings of Harvard researchers on the use of tranquilizers and sleeping pills in nursing homes and rest homes provide a glaring example of institutional impatience. To make "management" of patients easier and cheaper, half of those in the twelve nursing homes and fifty-five rest homes studied had been kept on the psychoactive drugs. Old prescriptions had not been evaluated for half the drug-receiving residents in a year, and often the staff members who were administering the drugs did not understand the purpose or the side effects of the medication. A bad habit had gotten entrenched.[32]

To advocate institutional embodiment of the virtues we have described is to advocate that institutions be covenantal and not merely contractual. Support for such a normative judgment can be derived from several sources. (1) The religious traditions to which many members of our society still give allegiance support such social organization. (2) The implicit or explicit charters of institutions to function in a society carry covenantal implications. Institutions are gifted even more than they are givers, and the recognition of what one owes is at the root of institutional responsibility. (3) What most of us have experienced in institutional conditions that do and do not nurture human flourishing, meet human need, and avoid human alienation should also lend support to the position.

Measuring Professional Responsibility

If a sense of covenant is the key to moral responsibility in organizations as institutions, it is also the crucial ingredient of moral responsibility in professions as institutions. May's emphasis on the physician's gratitude for gifts as the foundation of a professional covenant has relevance for all professions, especially for the helping professions in which hurting people place their trust. Physician Edmund Pellegrino underscores a professional's social contract rather than a covenant, but his rendition of contract pushes toward covenant. Consider the privileges helping professionals enjoy: to conduct experiments, to "practice" as neophytes, to be largely self-regulating, to receive privileged communication. His contract involves "fidelity to the promise to help."[33] The language of privilege, trust, and promise suggests a covenantal obligation more than a contractual bargain. Professionals' knowledge and skill are not mere personal acquisitions; they are societal resources. Whether we use a covenant or contract label is less critical than whether we see professions as what Robert Bellah and William Sullivan call "agencies of the common good" rather than only as means of personal advancement and profit. Professionals have a calling more than a career or a job.[34] A calling links a person to the community and its well-being.

As Pellegrino asserts, the callings that deal with health, knowledge, salvation, and justice especially demand going beyond self-interest to serve the wounded and vulnerable. But why not make a sense of obligation to serve the common good and a sense of one's knowledge and skill as a public and even a sacred trust the distinguishing marks of professionals? For instance, there is no reason why engineers, corporate managers, and accountants cannot feel such a calling. In the sea of complex problems and choices that we all must traverse, we often feel vulnerable and dependent on the assistance of trustworthy equivalents of boatwrights and navigators who are providers of goods and services. The coverage of "helping profession" could stretch well beyond those who minister to us in personal crises.

One of the privileges enjoyed by professionals is power, and power, of course, has a tendency to corrupt. Professionals with a covenantal understanding of their privileges and obligations will be reformers of professions as well as servants of the common good through professions. They will turn a critical eye on the effects of a profession's training on its practitioners and the exercise of power by them. As surely as a healthy organization needs built-in sedition, a health profession needs dissidents, or what Steven Murphy calls "resistant professionals."[35] These people will question the established versions of professional roles, buck senseless bureaucratic red tape, and sound the alarm when professionals become uncritical of the economic and political status quo. They will contradict the "power trip" mentality that reduces the people with whom the professional works to people on whom or over whom a professional works. I once saw a cartoon depicting a group of women in convent-style habits who were also wearing huge beaks on their heads. One of the nuns is saying to an inquiring outsider, "We are a pecking order." A covenantal perspective provides a needed corrective to the prevalent professional preoccupation with pecking orders.

Concern for the common good makes a profession out of a career, and a sense of sacred obligation makes a calling out of a profession. May reminds us that covenant has religious roots in both the biblical tradition and the Hippocratic tradition—an ultimate giver and obligator calls us to our service. People who do not think of themselves as called by God can still be professionals in the sense of agents of the common good, but Bellah and Sullivan rightly point to religious communities as offering the best promise for revitalizing the professions as servants of the public interest.[36]

Although the authors of *Habits of the Heart* seem to see institutions of higher education only as accomplices in the "professionalism without content" of the "managers" and "therapists" they describe, rather than as agents for the recovery of professions as callings, I hope they are wrong. Part of a good education should be not only preparation for citizenship but also a challenge to serve the public good through one's vocation. Communities of both faith and learning can help people discover a sense of calling.

Summary

This chapter has suggested normative measures of institutional morality or responsibility. We have traced stages of institutional moral development that would assist in assessing the depth of an institution's commitment to whatever values it espouses or evidences without saying what those values should be. Beyond that, we have advanced normative proposals for making institutions more responsible, not merely in relation to the values they espouse but in relation to values, obligations, and virtues that they should embody. Institutions can be considered more or less moral, based on evaluation of their purposes and consequences; their promulgated obligations as expressed in principles, rules, and rights; and their characteristic virtues. Institutions not only reflect and nurture virtues in individuals, but institutional structures, styles, and stories reflect and sustain corporate virtues. Finally, we have explored the recovery of a form of professionalism that serves the public good and turns careers into callings.

The virtues, ends, and obligations advocated here are rooted in a covenantal understanding of institutions that stretches the reach of covenantal obligation beyond the institution to a universal community encompassing animal life and the good earth as well as human membership. The covenant originates in indebtedness to others; it entails obligation to others; it is sustained by care and fidelity that seek to include universal community in the scope of concern. Institutions as such cannot be worshipers of an ultimate covenantal giver, but they can build in sedition to undermine the pretensions of anything else that bids for worship. As Andrew Hacker has insisted, every institution needs a vice president in charge of heresy, not to suppress it but to keep it alive.[37] The ethicist in institutional settings should remain the undomesticated gadfly who forever resists the institution's temptation to take itself too seriously and lobbies for institutional expressions of the self-critical role.

4
Imaginative Contexts: Metaphors, Images, and Models

Buz: "What's a metaphor?"

Cohn: "It's a symbol—sort of. It says something not fully expected, through analogy. . . . An object, because of a quality in common with another, is taken to represent the other. For instance, Walt Whitman in one of his poems, refers to the grass as 'the handkerchief of the Lord'—far out but reasonable. . . . It provides an earthly concept of God: He who walks on grass with the same ease as he uses His handkerchief. Or He may use the grass to wipe His brow. Anyway, He dwells in our lives. Another similar concept is God the Father."

Bernard Malamud, *God's Grace*

All moral behavior proceeds by metaphor.

Michael Ignatieff

In the beginning we create the enemy. Before the weapon comes the image. We *think* others to death and then invent the battle-axe or the ballistic missiles with which to actually kill them. Propaganda precedes technology.

Sam Keen, *The Face of the Enemy*

A local plant manager was visiting a college class on business ethics, and he was asked what he did when an effort is launched to unionize his plant. His reply was immediate: "We go to war." This church officer and devoted family man would not have sunk to activity that was illegal or that he considered unethical, but to him a successful campaign to unionize would be proof positive of his ineffectiveness as a manager. He was not going to take it lying down. By employing the war metaphor, he was illustrating the prevalence of that metaphor in our society.[1]

Wars and Games

From the locker room to the boardroom, from the basketball court to our day in court, and from the hospital halls to the halls of congress, we often think of ourselves as doing battle with an adversary. In the battle of the sexes, all is fair just as it is in war. We have price wars as well as military wars. The other party in the suit, the other party in the election, the other team, the competing company, the other contender for the position we want, the other school of thought, or the other fraternity or sorority is an enemy to be defeated. We also may battle oppression or the forces of evil. We may attack poverty, pollution, illiteracy, or disease. We often regard death as the ultimate enemy.

To think of any activity as war is to place it in a certain imaginative context and to make certain attitudes and actions appropriate because of that context. When the adversary is the enemy, not the friendly competition, then we tend to believe we must win at all costs. We must do to them before they do to us. Our thinking is dominated by the sense that, since someone or something is out to get us, we shall bar no holds, give no quarter, and take no prisoners. The wearer of the KILL A COMMIE FOR CHRIST button, the "jungle fighter" in the corporate world, and the pursuer of every legal angle in the divorce settlement may then have in common a demonized opponent and a feeling that only one of us is going to come out of this in good shape.

There may be a time and a place for going to war. The magnitude of the evil and the recalcitrance of the opposition may lead us to decide that the means for continuing the conflict must be militant and even military. In confronting the evil of racial segregation and oppression, Martin Luther King, Jr., would not resort to violence, yet he spoke of nonviolence as the most powerful "weapon" the movement had in its struggle. It was a war in that it was a clash of weapons, but leaders like King would not let the war mentality take over. The military metaphor did not become the reigning one because of a higher commitment to nonviolent resistance and love of the enemy.

When the enemy is death in the hospital or pollution in the environment or homelessness in the city or poverty any place, war seems to be an appropriate metaphor. It may be a comfort to know that the hospital staff is conducting an all-out campaign against one's disease—that is, unless the campaign comes to be more dreaded than the disease because one is being kept "alive" at all costs. A surgeon told one of my classes that he viewed death as the enemy that stalks the halls of the hospital. In *High Noon* shoot-out fashion, he described his battles with the enemy as struggles to the last gasp. A few minutes later, however, he contradicted himself. He recounted waiting until his sister could arrive from a distant city so that they together could make the decision about turning off the respirator that was breathing for their terminally ill, comatose parent. It turned out that the war metaphor was qualified or balanced by other images or metaphors of the doctor's role. The doctor as parent (and the son as doctor) made the decision rather than the doctor as fighter.

As the aging of our society pushes us toward greater attention to the care of the chronically ill, the metaphor of defeating or killing an invader (the disease) is clearly inappropriate. A Hastings Center Report special supplement on "Ethical Challenges of Chronic Illness" in 1988 suggested that diplomacy, with its attendant negotiation and reconciliation, is a better metaphor for attempts to cope with such conditions as arthritis, hearing impairment, and hypertension. The affected person is seeking to find meaning in life in spite of an illness that will not go away. Cure is not the issue; coexistence is.[2]

Living only by the war metaphor often causes problems elsewhere than in health care, even when the ends are noble. Magnificent obsessions, even those aimed at defeating or destroying some social ill, remain obsessions. They can easily lower us. We seek people and groups to blame and preclude the possibility that they may have some redeeming qualities. We succumb to a creeping blindness to the ambivalence of our motives and the mixed results of our actions. Questionable means and questionable consequences easily follow from crusades, even holy ones—especially holy ones. The saddest wars of all are religiously justified battles over doctrine, moral issues, political power, and economic interest. Bombing and blockading abortion clinics or terrorism in North Ireland or Iran's posture and actions toward "the Great Satan" should suffice for illustration. T. V. Smith once cautioned that there is "a little totalitarian operating in the bosom of every conscientious man, especially when he is a middle man operating in the name of God." To make matters worse, "There is nothing more trigger-happy than a hyperthyroid conscience."[3]

Use of military metaphors has adversely affected management styles in this country in more ways than the "jungle fighter" style. Karl Weick warns that organizing a corporation using a military model dictates that some will win and some will lose and limits the range of possibilities the manager can entertain. Only certain forms of organization and solutions to problems are thinkable.[4] As correctives for this rut, Thomas J. Peters and Robert H. Waterman, Jr., in *In Search of Excellence*, see the "best-run companies" experimenting with other management metaphors. Sailing, play, management by walking around, seesaws, structured chaos, space stations, and skunk works are but a few of the new images or styles they find.

Law students often feel torn by their discomfort with the metaphor of law as fighting. As James Foster discovers in his studies of fourteen students, women are often less able to be eager adversaries than men. If they adjust to being adversaries at all, they are "reluctant adversaries." For himself and for them, Foster asks, "Can reluctant adversaries succeed in a profession defined metaphorically by hating while also reshaping legal practice more along the lines of loving?"[5] The battling mentality one woman encountered caused her to object that the adversary process creates enemies instead of solving problems. Both women and men who feel this tension are faced with the options of going along and playing the adversarial game, of rejecting it and making themselves outsiders, or of attempting to do well professionally in the adversarial system but at the same time to connect with clients in a caring relationship that will attend to the person's feelings and needs, not just to the legal problem in question.[6] In Carol Gilligan's terms, these reluctant adversaries are trying to balance an ethic of rights and an ethic of care.

Fortunately, all of us do not regard all life's competitions as wars. Some of them are friendly and restrained. In fact, even some military encounters have been carried on with a measure of restraint and respect for the opponent that made genuine peace more likely and more lasting. "It is all in the game" often means "Watch out." But "It's only a game" means we can appreciate adversaries as competitors who bring out our best efforts and highest accomplishments. In our justice system, litigation does not have to ruin either party, and attorneys can respect the challenges they present to each other and even remain friends despite being opponents. Rival candidates can be constructive challengers to each other rather than contenders in a demolition derby. Athletes can respect and appreciate each other across the scrimmage line, the net, and the diamond. Business competitors can view their endeavors as a game[7] and enjoy plotting strategies and making points without taking a "them or us" approach. Family disagreements can be friendly debates rather than vicious exchanges. Academic arguments can be times of mutual learning instead of skirmishes leading to lasting animosities. But as long as a war metaphor dominates the way we conceive any of these encounters, we meet on hostile terms. If a game metaphor or some other metaphor provides the image through which we view the situation, the terms are different.

Metaphors, Images, Models, Stories, and Myths

Institutions, which have been our focus in the past two chapters, are carriers of metaphors, images, stories, and myths. In *In Search of Excellence*, Peters and Waterman reveal not only that the exemplary companies are value driven but also that metaphors, images, stories, and myths are prominent and powerful means for the communication of those values.[8] All organizations and professions use metaphors (speaking of one thing in terms of another) and images (mental pictures) to understand themselves, present themselves to outsiders, and orient members in their cultures. An institution may use several different metaphors to support a particular image of itself for both internal and public effect. "Reach out and touch someone." "The good hands people." "Justice is blind." "The minister is a shepherd to the flock." "A helping profession." "Our college is a family."

These metaphors and images are often imbedded in the stories we tell about ourselves, and how our institution was started, about the heroes and "characters" of our institution's story. In Bernard Malamud's *God's Grace*, Cohn, the lone human survivor of a nuclear holocaust, is asked by Buz, the chimpanzee who is his fellow survivor, where stories came from. When Cohn answers that they came from other stories, Buz asks where they (the earlier stories) came from. Cohn says, "Somebody spoke a metaphor and that broke into a story. Man had to tell them to keep his life from washing away."[9] "People imagine their world into being," as Sharon Parks tells us.[10] Metaphors break into stories, but it can work the other way too: stories get distilled into metaphors and images. William F. May observes, "An image tells a kind of compressed story, not a particular story about an identifiable person, nor an exemplary tale designed to inspire, but a prototypical story to which all specific narratives bear a family resemblance."[11] A story about a person that seems to capture that person's character or personality may provide an image or metaphor of that person for other people. Both stories and metaphors are everywhere in our social world, and both provide us with lenses for perceiving current experience and projecting our futures. We are virtually speechless without them, for without them experience would be a roar of undifferentiated stimuli.

For our purposes, the words *metaphor* and *image* will often be used interchangeably, but models are different. Models are also metaphorical, but a model is a dominant, established metaphor. Sallie McFague explains, "[A] model is a metaphor with 'staying power.' A model is a metaphor that has gained sufficient stability and scope so as to present a pattern for relatively comprehensive and coherent explanations."[12] She uses as her prime example the metaphor of God as father in traditional Christian theology. Models tempt us to forget that they are metaphors.

Ian Barbour pushes further than McFague in defining *model* and makes its distinction from metaphor clearer. Models, he suggests, are "imaginative tools for ordering experience." Models use selected aspects of complex systems to shed light on a subject or problem. We have models of economic development or population growth, for example. We also use models to explain God's relation to the world. Barbour discusses five such models, which are analogous to (1) an absolute monarch's relation to a kingdom (the closest model to the patriarchal one rejected by McFague), (2) a clock-maker's relation to a clock, (3) one person's relation to another person, (4) an agent's relation to her or his own actions, and (5) the relation of a preeminent member of a society to the rest of the society. Each of these is metaphor, but while a metaphor is employed momentarily to enlarge or transform our vision, a model is systematically developed. It is constructed and elaborated to simplify and explain. Models, as Barbour explains them, result from systematic reflection on myths, which articulate significant meaning in narrative form. Thus the models of God's relation to the world are selectively derived from myths, which are particular kinds of stories.[13]

Myth, like *model*, is a word that could bog us down interminably in definitional hassles. Myths mean misconceptions in much common usage, and certainly myths have perpetrated many of them. Nevertheless, myths are better understood as ways of seeing the world. For our purposes here, let us use Elisabeth Schüssler Fiorenza's capsule designation: "a story that provides a common vision."[14]

For some people, the term *myth* is best limited to stories about the origins of things, such as Babylonian and Hebrew creation stories. Barbour speaks of myth as "a story which is taken to manifest some aspect of the cosmic order" and which provides "a vision of the basic structure of reality."[15] As his definitions imply, myths do provide foundations of religion, but Barbour admits that modern secular philosophies are mythic also, even though they include no divine beings in their casts of characters. Babylonian and Hebrew creation stories are myths, but we shall not confine the term to such stories of sacred origins.

Joseph Campbell uses the narrower definition in calling a myth a "mask of God" and "a metaphor for what lies beyond the visible world." For that reason he considered our era devoid of valid mythology, and he believed it would be a long time before we could have a mythology because "things are changing too fast to become mythologized."[16] Yet when he observes what all myths have always dealt with—the maturation of the individual, the person's relation to society, and the society's relation to the world of nature and the cosmos—we must in turn argue that people still situate themselves in these ways. The myths we live by may be piecemeal, they may lack a mystical dimension, and they may be a diluted mixture of leftovers that nourish poorly if at all, but we still have them.

Myths often badly misrepresent or distort reality, but we must all rely on some myth or worldview or story that sets our lives in some larger context of meaning. Daniel Maguire observes, "Good minds under the influence of the myth [in this instance 'the woman myth'] reached preposterous conclusions with no qualms."[17] Every myth, he rightly insists, needs criticism because it cannot capture all truth, but he also rightly acknowledges that we are bound to sort out our experience using some myth or myths, understood as worldviews. Therefore we cannot step out of our mythic and storied locations and launch criticisms of our myths and those of others from some detached, objective standpoint. The critique, then, will either occur within a shared myth from the perspective of those who understand it differently or in conversation within other mystic orientations that teach us to see ourselves to some extent as they do.

Stories, myths, and worldviews, like metaphors, images, and models, are part of the contexts in which we function as moral beings and providers of contact lenses for interpretation of situations we inhabit and encounter. We live in them, and they live in us. They are both points of contact and points of view, and we shall consider them in the next chapter.

To say that we imagine our world using metaphors, images, stories, and myths is not to say that the biosphere is a figment of our imaginations. There is a ready-made world out there that we have not created. Oceans, rocks, trees, people, ozone layers, and acid rain are there, and we have to come to terms with them. Yet we also imagine them. Our metaphors, models, stories, worldviews, and institutions mediate our awareness, our neglect, our appreciation, and our exploitation of the natural and social world around us. We inhabit a universe of discourse that society has provided to give order and meaning to the physical universe. What we experience as reality is a social construction.[18] Life's setting has not been the same for everybody in every time and place and social membership. To deal with ethical issues adequately, we must become more aware of the imaginative filters with which we characterize ourselves and others and with which we sort out the ethical challenges we face.

Covenant as Metaphor, Model, and Myth

Our earlier discussion of institutions as contexts of ethics brought numerous metaphors into play, but the metaphors of contract and covenant took on major importance. Covenant has emerged as a more promising metaphor and model than contract for filtering our perceptions of institutions and making them more morally responsible. Granted it is more promising because it expresses a worldview in which we feel at home because of our religious, national, professional, or institutional identifications, it still addresses aspects of people's shared experience about which they can converse across

the fences that separate our imaginative habitats.[19] Thinking of organizations or professions in covenantal terms gives us a particular
perception of them and places us in a different context than if we
use different metaphors or models. Covenant is a metaphor that at
times has become a model and that expresses an overarching myth
or worldview.

H. Richard Niebuhr, in his article "The Idea of Covenant and
American Democracy,"[20] points out that the ideas people hold
about themselves, their societies, and their place in the universe
often parallel one another. Their ethics, their politics, and their religion often influence one another. In the Middle Ages, people regarded the self, the society, and the cosmos as hierarchies. In the
self, reason was on top, and the will and emotions were subordinate.
In the society, the pecking order ran from kings to serfs. In the
cosmos, it ran from God and the angels to animals and inanimate
things. In the eighteenth century a mechanical metaphor became
the model. The universe, the society, and the self were seen as machines. God was the watchmaker; natural laws make society, nature,
and human nature rational organizations. A pervasive nineteenth-
and twentieth-century metaphor has been the field of forces. Freud-
ian psychology depicted the dynamic struggle of id, ego, and super-
ego and highlighted the irrational and subconscious forces that
shape and move us. Domestic and world politics and economics
were seen as welters of competing interests and countervailing powers. The corresponding cosmic vision sees a dynamic and even tu-
multuous evolutionary process unfolding. What appear to be fixed
and static entities, such as tables, are actually dynamic bundles of
energy. Everything is in flux and nothing is nailed down.

In a similar way, covenant was a powerful and pervasive metaphor
and model when our nation was founded and fashioned. A covenantal people believed that they had unlimited responsibility to and for
one another and for the common laws under God. Personal identity,
political order, and religion were imagined as covenantal, based on
mutual promises and commitments, rather than merely natural
(based on blood and soil) or contractual (based on common interests). Natural and contractual bonds were prevalent too, and, in
some readings of the American experiment, a contractual understanding of society has always held the upper hand, but for Niebuhr,
covenant was the predominant model.

Of course, the source of this metaphor that became a model was
the Bible. As Walter Brueggemann puts it, "Biblical faith is essen-
tially covenantal in its perception of reality."[21] It presents covenant making as the primary human activity and provided the
mythic framework for many people's worldviews when our nation
was young. The Hebrews derived the covenant metaphor from

treaty arrangements in their political environment, and it came to dominate their theology, their sociology, and their psychology. It was their myth. The individual person's identity and well-being were inextricably bound up with life in community, and community life was ordered and maintained by covenantal obligations and promises.

Basing human relationships on contracts has a long history and widespread allegiance as well. Focused on the protection of the individual's rights and interests, contracts provide explicit guarantees that parties to the bargain do not take advantage of one another. The metaphor and model of contract has been invaluable as a protection of individual interests of employees and parties.to business transactions, but its coverage seems to have oozed into every aspect of contemporary life in our society. Under its dominance every relationship, every political affiliation, every religious affiliation, every marriage, and every job tends to be subjected to constant examination to determine whether it is paying off. Instead of entering into permanent covenantal commitments to continue through thick and thin, people make tentative, temporary, guarded agreements and keep their eyes on the exits. If I am not getting all out of this arrangement that I ought to be getting out of it, it is time to shop for something better. So covenants sink to contracts. We are talking about more than the conflict of metaphors; we are talking about the clash of myths as we shall see in the next chapter.

Framing Problems Metaphorically

Now that we have sorted out some terms, it is time to look at some of the implications of our imaginative contexts of ethics. The wrong metaphors can create blinders to moral problems and enable us to escape responsibility, but apt metaphors and images can shape character and illumine choice in positive ways. They have this dual potential because we inevitably frame problems with them. We see ourselves and others in a particular light, and we see society, nature, and whatever gods we acknowledge with a telling slant.

Donald Schon has examined the importance of metaphors for "problem setting" in social policy. Metaphors are crucial for two reasons: they are both perspectives or ways of looking at things (products) and introducers of new perspectives on problems (processes). "Problem settings are mediated . . . by the 'stories' people tell about troublesome situations—stories in which they describe what is going on and what needs fixing." The potential of these stories for assisting with the solution of problems is usually found in the generative metaphors contained in the stories. He cites the example of different generative metaphors people have used to look at inner-city housing problems. As long as planners used the metaphor of blight and renewal, the appropriate action was the removal of the blight and the redesign of the entire area. On the other hand, if a "slum" includes a natural community of belonging and comfort, a genuine neighborhood, then a strategy of reinforcing the positive features of the situation and rehabilitation of the area makes sense.[22] "Problem setting" in this case becomes crucial for problem solving because certain remedies will follow from particular metaphorical settings of the problem. If we want to address the problem, we have to do more than gather "facts"; we must contrast metaphors. As long as our approach is shaped by a particular metaphor or images, we will screen out counterindications.

Consider the way dominant images and metaphors influence our diagnosis of the hunger problem in the world. Each of the images implies elevation of particular values and advocacy for particular courses of action. The lifeboat image, which has been used by Garrett Hardin, among others, makes survival the dominant consideration and assumes that survival is not possible for everyone.[23] Beginning from the disputed premise that there is not enough food to go around and there never will be, proponents of the lifeboat metaphor have pictured the food-rich nations as occupants of a seagoing craft of limited capacity and the food-poor nations as dead in the water if they are not taken on board by the shipshape nations. To take everyone on would mean ultimately that the haves would sink with the have-nots because the lifeboat cannot hold everyone.

The image or metaphor of food as a weapon has been touted by Henry Kissinger and some subsequent policymakers in our government and in governments of other food-rich nations. Food-poor nations may do the same, withholding relief from areas where political opposition is concentrated. National security now assumes center stage as the highest value, and food becomes first and foremost a means to advance the national interest by rewarding military allies and punishing non-allies. People then become pawns on an international geopolitical chessboard, and the weakest suffer the most because they are least able to make it hard on us if we do not come to their aid.

The image of the birth-control device often frames the problem for those who view the hunger problem as primarily a population problem. In this case survival may again be a central value, if overpopulation is regarded as the potential sinker of the whole boat we inhabit, but individual freedom and responsibility (of persons and nations) is probably even more prominent. If hunger follows overpopulation and people are given the information and the technology to limit their birthrates, then it is their responsibility, not ours, according to this position, if they cannot feed themselves. Fixation on birth control thus blinds us to deeper economic, social, and religious roots of overpopulation.

The image of "the green revolution" has attracted considerable support in the past, and new versions of faith in technological fixes continue to emerge. If we put a high premium on avoiding any current curtailment of our standard of living or any adjustment in our way of life, we often take refuge in the assumption that science and technology will come up with solutions to food-production problems caused by the rapid shrinkage of arable land due to everything from desertification to urban sprawl.

The image of the Christmas basket or the "We Are the World" record benefit has a large following. With the central value of charity or compassion, the special offering and telethon approach has elicited heartening and helpful levels of generosity. Temporary relief has saved thousands of lives and assuaged horrible suffering, but long-term solutions do not necessarily follow in the wake of short-term palliatives. As one person put it, "Relief measures are teaspoons," and they are also spoon-feeding. The best help helps people help themselves.

Dennis Shoemaker once suggested the metaphor of the tilted billiard table for imagining the problem of world hunger.[24] Compensatory justice emerges as the primary value or principle implied by this image. The billiard table is the global economy. Because of trade arrangements, debt levels, economies centered on a very few natural resources or crops for export due to international markets, and location of the chief assets of capital and technology, poorer nations have played on a tilted table. Most of the balls end up rolling into the same pockets, those of the developed, affluent nations. Only a different tilt on loans, land reform, and use of energy can get more of the balls rolling into different pockets. A new international economic order is needed.

Two final images are the "spaceship earth" of Kenneth Boulding[25] and the "global village" of Marshall McLuhan.[26] Here solidarity or community is the chief underlying value or principle. Here "We Are the World" is not just a song to finance relief, but an alliance to found reconciliation. This image envisions everyone in the same boat in an interdependent world. With this outlook, survival is a shared problem of the village, not a protection project of the haves on the hill.

World hunger is but one of many problems we envision using images and metaphors with decided ethical and political ramifications. In her article "Ethics and the Language of AIDS,"[27] Judith Wilson Ross lays out a range of metaphors that have appeared in discussions of AIDS and that reveal how dangerous the metaphors that shape our perception can be. AIDS had been equated with death personified. Instead of being seen as a spectrum disease with a wide range of effects, AIDS is the grim reaper out looking for victims. For some, gay sex has become equated with death, because it is high-risk activity for the transmission of AIDS. The ethical, medical, and political upshot of the death metaphor may be to regard those with the virus as already dead and to regard treatment and financial assistance as useless.

The punishment metaphor is also prevalent. Because homosexual intercourse and illegal IV drug use account for 90 percent of the transmissions in the United States, AIDS is called God's judgment or nature's retribution on those who engage in these activities. The hemophiliacs, other recipients of blood transfusions, and children of female AIDS patients who make up the other 10 percent are the "innocent victims"; the rest are guilty victims who are often treated with less sympathy in hospitals, in public agencies, and in news media. If I do not approve of your behavior and your suffering can be linked to that behavior, then you no longer have my sympathy. Other suffering caused by psychological makeup or unhealthy habits and choices may still evoke my compassion, but not *this* kind.

The crime and criminal metaphor sees AIDS as a serial killer claiming victims, and the person with AIDS may come to be regarded as a criminal as well. To fight this "crime" or "criminal," drastic steps will be necessary. Because of this "crime wave," quarantines, violations of privacy, and aggressive detective work may seem as necessary as increased expenditures. As Ross states, steps may exceed "the ordinary bounds of good sense, good law, and good ethics." The war metaphor is similar to the crime metaphor in its tendency to make the sufferer rather than the disease the enemy. If people "harbor" the virus even unknowingly and pass it on, they are like spies in our midst. The more we see the effort to prevent and cure AIDS as a war, the more people's feelings and rights can be contravened in the name of protecting society.

Ross's final metaphor is otherness, which she considers both the most difficult to illustrate and perhaps the most pervasive. AIDS happens to "them." They are different from us in the general population. It is not "our" problem except as "they" might pose a threat to "us." In this way, we may consider ourselves somehow immune from being touched by the disease personally or in our families and circles of friends. We can then believe it is not our problem. By contrast, the plague metaphor puts us both together under a common threat from a common enemy. From the metaphor flows the morality. From better metaphors, better ethics and better public policy can emerge.

Another example of metaphoric problem setting for social and institutional policy is the evolution of images for a college's or university's relationship to its students. Until the 1960s a pervasive metaphor was in loco parentis. The college was the guardian of the morals of the young in their home away from home. Probably no school went so far as to remove "any known form of sin" fifteen miles from its campus, as one college allegedly claimed, but paternalism was the order of the day. Then came the demands for student rights by people who figured that you ought to get to make some decisions about your residence-hall visitation hours and your consumption of alcohol if you were old enough to die in Vietnam. Student rights became the dominant image or model. More recently the model of contract has gained the dominant position, with the students and parents as consumers, the educational institution as the seller and provider, and the lawyers available on call. Here and there different metaphors have been normative, such as the image of shared responsibility in community. All of these metaphoric frames of reference elevate different values and lead in different directions for an institution's culture and governance. Finding the right metaphor or model is even more critical than developing a better set of policies.

A metaphoric struggle is currently in progress over how we should imagine our organizational structures for communication and decision making. According to John Naisbitt in *Megatrends,* the network is in the process of replacing the pyramid.[28] Forward-looking organizations are flattening their hierarchies to enhance collaboration and broaden participation. Robert Reich sees hierarchies shrinking with the growth of professional partnerships, teamwork, and collective entrepreneurship, but the perennial attachment of corporations to the pyramid metaphor is not being given up without a fight.[29] The implications of the shift for communication flow and collaborative creativity are obvious, but there are others. *Women's Ways of Knowing* observes that with pyramids there are winners and losers. Some get to be top dogs, and some are consigned to underdog status. With webs and nets as our guiding images, connections are not hierarchical, and win/win collaboration is possible. The metaphors have a moral.

On the level of personal decision making, metaphors and images can be great problem setters and solution suggesters. At the risk of making a choice too simple, they can at times help us to cut through all the underbrush and get our bearings. A friend of mine once told me a career decision he made using images or metaphors. During the tensest days of the movement for school desegregation in a certain Southern city, this minister had become too visible in support of civil rights to suit his congregation's board of officers. After a confrontation at a meeting of the officers, he resigned, not knowing what his next work would be. Within the next few weeks, three opportunities presented themselves. One friend, not even knowing that this man was out of work, told him that he wanted him to be a troubleshooter with his corporation, a solid and growing company with numerous branches. Very soon after that offer was tendered, another friend called to say that this man's services were desired as the executive secretary of the state human relations council, the most active interracial body at work in the state on the issues that claimed his commitment and brought the termination of his employment with the congregation he had been serving. A bit later, still another friend called to tell him that his denomination's regional director of Christian education in that state had resigned and he was the person the church wanted to see as the successor.

All three positions were enticing. All three would enable him to use his talents and follow his concerns. The decision became more and more complicated. Finally he arrived at an image or metaphor for each opportunity. For the corporate position, he imagined a blazer with a club coat of arms on it. He could see himself enjoying entree not only to boardrooms but also to clubhouses in numerous cities in this country and abroad. His financial future would be assured, and he would be working for a respected organization and for a friend he admired. For the human relations council position, he imagined a knight on a white horse. He would be clearly aligned with the movement for racial justice and needed social change in his area. He would probably have to take a great deal of flak, but he would know that he was on the right side. For the position in the denomination's organizational bureaucracy (or network), he imagined a mother, his mother church, the womb that had given him life, the bosom that had nurtured him. There would be a lot of tedium, but he would be helping mother church keep her house in order and nurture her children and adults in the faith. The images defined the issues for him better than lists of pros and cons had done.

Images of the Self as Professional

My friend was wrestling with alternative images of himself as much as with representative metaphors or images for the positions. Images of ourselves are laden with moral significance as surely as images of social problems are. These images may be either images connected to certain roles that we discharge (the good doctor, the good husband or wife, the good student, the good citizen, the good employee) or images intended to capture the posture and practice of a person in all phases of life (the winner, the victim, the servant, the free spirit). Both deserve further examination.

William F. May's book *The Physician's Covenant* probes the ethical implications of several images of the physician. The parent image carries the favorable freight of self giving and compassion. It affirms the values of order and nurture. However, parentalism also slips into paternalism—the managerial approach that knows best what is good for the patient and may ride roughshod over the patient's wishes or never explore them in the first place.

The fighter image has heroic and tragic expressions. This courageous healer salvages cases that some consider hopeless, but fighters also may not know when to quit. Fighters can be so obsessed with staving off death that they extract a lamentable human cost in the process. They can also give diminished attention to care when cure ceases to be a possibility.

The skilled technician awes us with expertise and upholds the highest standards for the profession, but the patient can become virtually an occasion for a performance. The person may be missed by the pro who makes a surgical strike on the ailment and moves to the next challenge.

Arguing from an acknowledged Christian orientation, May elevates the images of the covenanted healer and the teacher. The two merge because the covenanted healer will be willing to take the time teaching requires to assist people to be healthy. The covenant image is normative for May. All the images imply virtues the healer needs, but the covenantal image provides a critique of the strengths and weaknesses of the others.

Michael Maccoby's *The Gamesman,* and *Full Value,* by Oliver Williams and John Houck, examine some images of corporate managers.[30] In the Maccoby study of the executive model in the electronics industry, it is not the dog-eat-dog jungle fighter, not the single-minded skill practitioner (the craftsman), not the team-playing company person, but the "gamesman" who represents the state of the art. This executive loves the challenge of pulling off deft maneuvers within the rules of the game to best, but not destroy, the rival coach. The executive skilled in "gamesmanship" is constantly plotting new strategies for new contests. The money, the technical expertise, and the company identification are less important than repeated salvages of risky situations as this player jumps from challenge to challenge. Lee Iacocca is often mentioned as the quintessential gamesman.

Each of the images suffers from crippling, if not always fatal, flaws. The jungle fighter turns business into war, and, should that person attempt to follow a different image at home or church, the ensuing compartmentalized life is ruinous to personal integrity. The craft ace risks a different brand of compartmentalization. Tunneled into a professional niche, this person may miss the corporate forest amid the trees of the trade. Craftspeople may become oblivious to the institutional impact of their endeavors (in engineering, for example) and

impotent to effect institutional change. The company person may
work so hard at blending into the team that she or he makes no
waves, introduces no diversity, and ventures no criticism. The
strongest teams, however, would not encourage such acquiescence.
The "gamesman" gets Maccoby's highest marks, but he diagnoses a
split in the operator's personality that should set off the alarms. It is
a separation of the heart and the head. A cool operator in "the
game," this executive often has trouble with the warmth and vulnerability that go with getting close to people.

Houck and Williams assess each of Maccoby's types (substituting
"the king on the mountain" for the jungle fighter) and add others.
"Millionaires" have the drive and cunning to accomplish their monetary goals, but they neglect the needs of others and the claims of
justice. "The captain on the bridge" has the politician's flexibility,
but lacks the statesman's idealism. The master image advanced from
the Bible is the heir of the kingdom of God, which Houck and Williams discuss in combination with the servant of the Lord and the
pilgrim people of God. This heir will deal very differently with in-
competent managers and burned-out employees than would a king
on the mountain because the heir has a different view of the leader's
position, of personnel, and of life's benefits. The heir cares about
what can be done for employees, not just about what they can or
cannot do for the company.

In *A Passion for Excellence: The Leadership Difference*, Thomas
Peters and Nancy Austin discuss some new metaphors of corporate
leadership.[31] The old order has changed. The cop, the devil's advocate, the naysayer, and the pronouncer are giving way to the cheer-
leader, the coach, the teacher, the facilitator, and the nourisher. A
good coach counsels, confronts, sponsors, and educates along with
the coaching. Robert Reich, in *Tales of a New America*, sees "collective entrepreneurship" as the wave of the future rather than "the
Triumphant Individual," the hero of one of America's hardy perennial morality tales. Japan's "loyal teammate" is replacing the rugged
individual. Team triumphs and Nobel prizes to groups are signs of
new times.[32]

Peters and Austin commend a second set of images, primarily because managers in successful companies operate according to them.
Reich pushes the team concept because older versions of entrepreneurship are out of step with an increasingly interdependent world
in which our images of conflict and domination are serving us badly.
Reich's is a moral argument as well as a pragmatic one, and we
would push it further. Which images or metaphors either reflect or
imply the highest level of respect for people's dignity and concern
for their development? Being image-conscious is a priority for ethics
as well as for public relations, but the ethicist must ask what an

image makes of us and others, rather than what the image makes us appear to be.

Every professional role has its images and metaphors, and they all carry moral freight. Lawyers take the roles of defender, prosecuter, and judge. What values are implicit in those roles and in the system into which those roles fit? Lawyers may see themselves as entrepreneurs (logging the most hours in the firm each year and attaining financial goals), as game-players or hired guns (exploring every ploy and strategy the rules will allow to win another victory), as technicians (versed in all the details of the law), as officers of the court (discharging a necessary function within the system with a minimum of personal emotional involvement), as advocates for the endangered (representing the poor, those whose health has been damaged by asbestos or some other hazard in the workplace, those on death row, the interests of a corporation, or those of the environment), as counselors (assisting people through times of personal difficulty), or as guardians of the system of justice (maintaining the fairness and efficiency of the system to serve justice and the common good).

These images and roles matter morally. All good does not reside in one list of roles while all evil lodges with some others, but the images and roles do direct people's efforts in morally significant ways. They give a particular slant to their vision of themselves and their clients. And which masters we serve—as advocates, for instance—also matters morally. If we must compartmentalize our lives because the dominant professional metaphor is so alien to our personal values, we are robbing ourselves of integrity and living a contradiction that can be sustained only by self-delusion. Total immersion in the demands of the profession that leaves us no place to stand to criticize or evalute is damaging to the person, and ultimately corrosive of the profession.[33]

Members of the clergy may function primarily as pastors, preachers, resource managers, staff administrators, educators, leaders of social service and action, counselors, and various combinations of those and other roles. Within and among those roles, they may see themselves as facilitators, scholars, comforters of the afflicted, persons who afflict the comfortable, diplomats, fund-raisers, change agents, builders of ecumenical bridges, carriers of tradition, links to the larger denomination, organizers, and advocates for certain causes. How people in ministry see themselves and how others see them deserve periodic unpacking to discover what values are implicit in the priorities and commitments embedded in the roles people play.

Turning to the academic community, in a presentation at the 1987 Annual Meeting of the American Academy of Religion, David E. Smith and Charles Reynolds delineated and examined four images of faculty and administrative leadership in higher education. The "clinical expert" focuses on established procedures and seeks to make them work effectively. The "engaged reformer" is guided by certain principles or some vision of the common good. The "campus shepherd" is the transmitter and perpetuator of the institution's story. The "conscientious exemplar" embodies and elevates certain personal virtues. Each of these taken alone and taken to the extreme can be institutional liabilities, but each combined with the others and practiced at its best contributes to institutional strength. These types or images are useful in analyzing a variety of institutions and a variety of positions within institutions.

Professors may operate from images of themselves as scholarly, objective experts in their particular slices of a discipline, as passionate exponents of some school of thought, as therapeutic aids to student development, as efficient trainers in vocational skills, or as stimulating catalysts of liberating encounters. In *Women's Ways of Knowing*, Mary Field Belenky and her colleagues offer three sets of images of the teacher: the authority who dispenses knowledge, the referee who simply moderates student exchanges of ideas, and the midwife, coach, or partner who is intimately involved in dialogue with students.[34] The first exercises power, the second abdicates responsibility, and the third empowers students by the practice of forbearance. By forbearance, they mean withholding judgment long enough to allow the other's voice to be heard. The student correlate to each of the types of teachers is, in the first case, the receptacle or spectator, in the second case, the mere expresser of feelings who observes no discipline, and, in the third case, the ally or partner in dialogue and quest. There not only are academic differences here; there are also moral differences.

Integrating Images of the Self

Because we all fill several roles and feel the pull of a variety of images, we face the problem of finding the metaphor, the self-image, that will provide integrity and purpose for our lives as a whole. Amid the babble of voices telling us what to be and the variety of roles we are expected to play or want to play, what image of ourselves gives us our sense of identity? Are we playing out scripts in which we are characteristically the victim or the survivor, the winner or the loser, the connoisseur of the good things of life or the crusader for causes, the seeker for meaning or the servant of others, the aggressor or the peacekeeper?

The victim-survivor question, for instance, carries crucial importance in the lives of people who have been abused, raped, and subjected to other forms of persecution and cruelty, such as the Nazi death camps. When people continue to think of themselves as victims, they assume they will be mistreated by others and may frequently tolerate situations and relationships in which they are victimized. They are then defined by what others do to them. They feel destined to absorb the blows, to roll with the punches, to be put down. Survivors, on the other hand, interpret the same experiences differently. They refuse to allow themselves to be defined or controlled by what others have done to them. Rather, they regard themselves as people who have somehow prevailed despite what others have done. They retain a level of self-respect and assertiveness that enables them to reject humiliating situations and walk away from them.

From a long list of possibilities, we shall explore three images of the self.[35] All three enjoy both religious and secular support; all three can be manifestations of biblical faith; all three have positive expressions; and all three have questionable features if taken alone and taken to an extreme.

The first two are the servant and the liberated person, one exalting self-denial and the other self-fulfillment or self-actualization.[36] If they are Christians, the heaviest underlines in the servants' Bibles are found under Matthew 16:24 (RSV, alt.): "[Those who] would come after me, let [them] deny [themselves] and take up a cross and follow me." The text of choice for liberated persons might be John 10:10: "I came that they may have life, and have it abundantly." At the risk of caricature, we can draw some contrasts. For the servant, salvation is conceived in terms of subordination; for the liberated person, it is conceived in terms of self-realization. For the first, one is saved by surrender; for the second, through growth. On the one hand, holiness is obedience; on the other, it is wholeness. The first believes that self-denial is necessary to the love of God and others; the second that self-love is necessary to the love of any other. The slogan of one is "I am willing to be third." For the other, it is "I have to be myself." Says one, "The more I forget myself, the more I do God's will." Says the other, "The more I find myself, the more I feel God's presence in me."

Self-centeredness is the root sin in the first type, but the second enjoins us to be good to ourselves and to feel good about ourselves. For the first, the Spirit of God needs to descend, to fall upon a person or group, melting, molding, filling, and using, as the old song puts it. For the second, the Spirit is already present within us or is the totality of us. We need only realize what is already in us and act on its power. One may confess: "We have offended against Thy holy law. . . . [T]here is no health in us, . . . miserable offenders." The other may profess: "I am O.K. I feel good about myself."

Erich Fromm would label these "authoritarian religion" in the first instance and "humanistic religion" in the second.[37] In Fromm's version of authoritarian religion, God is the sole possessor of the reason and love that originally belonged to humanity. The more goodness God possesses, the less humanity has. In this zero-sum game, the fall is alienation from the God to whom all goodness is ascribed, leaving people with nothing but sin. Conversely, God in humanistic religion is the image of the person's higher self, a symbol of what we are or ought to become. The fall, then, is alienation from ourselves. It is obvious from these characterizations where Fromm's sympathies lie, but those on the self-denial side would reject his authoritarian label as unfair and deride his humanistic model as an even more unacceptable extreme.

Feminist theologians have pointed out that traditional views of sin as disobedience and insubordination have tended to reinforce the "rightness" of the traditional women's role. Women's attempts to realize their potentialities, assume greater public responsibility, and reject subordination are therefore "out of line" for religious reasons. Some feminists have finally given up on Judaism and Christianity for this very reason. The sexism and patriarchalism seem incorrigible. Others have reexamined the biblical traditions to separate the cultural blindness of the societies and writers whom we meet in the Bible from the breakthroughs toward human liberation that emerge there.

At its best, the servant image produces lives of unselfish service; at its worst it leads to groveling masochism. At its best, the liberated person image produces lives that realize more of the person's noblest and most creative potentialities; at its worst, it becomes expansive narcissism. Within the family context, we can cite parents who willingly and gladly deny themselves so that their children may have greater opportunities. We can also cite the manipulative martyrdom of parents who seek to control their offspring and justify their own existence by constant reminders of their thankless sacrifice. Conversely, we rejoice when daughters and sons resist conformity to stultifying parental prescriptions for their futures, insisting that they must discover what is right for them. But we also cringe when sons and daughters ride roughshod over parents' feelings in their preoccupation with their own self-expression.

In their most extreme state, the self-deniers say, "I don't matter," while the self-actualizers "look out for Number One." One says, "If I want it, it must be wrong." The other contends, "If I want it, it must be right." On the one hand, self-fulfillment equals selfishness; on the other, self-sacrifice equals sickness. Thus compassion becomes a complex for one and a trap for the other. For the self-deniers, the natural may be seen as the sinful; for the liberated, the natural may be equated with the sacred. In the first approach, people may simply accept oppressive situations because they are the cross God has given; for the second, people should find their identities only in themselves. At bottom, we have the yawning gap between "I am nothing" and "I am everything."

When they sink to these lows, these two approaches to life have a common predicament. Both the self-denial of the servant and the self-actualization of the liberated person are in danger of beginning and ending with self. If we become preoccupied with either our self-denial or our self-actualization rather than with what has claimed our service or what we are liberated for, we are preoccupied with ourselves. In human relationships, we should expect *mutual satisfaction* instead of treatment as doormats and *mutual sacrifice* instead of uninterrupted occupancy in the driver's seat. On the political front, we often acquiesce too passively to authority in our self-denial and abdicate too readily our public responsibility in our drive toward self-realization. In both instances, we become apolitical and therefore align ourselves with the status quo. True servanthood finds itself in what it serves; true liberation frees us for commitment to others.

Søren Kierkegaard gets at the basic kinship between the two extremes in *The Sickness Unto Death.*[38] Despair is "the sickness unto death," and there is a despair of weakness and a despair of strength. Being "not willing to be oneself" is the despair of weakness; "willing desperately to be oneself" is the despair of strength. Both are despair, which Kierkegaard presents as the fundamental human sin.

Are the way of the servant and the way of the liberated person reconcilable? Can the gap between them be closed without obscuring the creative tension between the two at their best? The Matthew and John texts might help when placed in context. The statement in Matthew about leaving self behind is followed by the assurance that people will find their true selves if they lose themselves for Jesus' sake. The statement in John about having life in all its fullness is set in the midst of a description of the good shepherd who lays down his life for his sheep.

Each image has something to offer the other one. From the servants we need to hear that only loved people can love themselves, and from the liberated we need to hear that if we do not love ourselves we must not believe we are loved. In our self-denial we need to remember that suffering is not necessarily caring, even though caring often brings suffering. "If I give away all I have, and if I deliver my body to be burned, but have not love, I gain nothing" (1 Cor. 13:3). In our self-actualizing, we need to know that caring means willingness to suffer, even though willingness to suffer does not guarantee that we care.

Both the servant and the liberated person have a message for professionals who are preoccupied with their status rather than dedicated to their calling. These professionals "don't do windows." By contrast, servants do what needs to be done if the institution or cause or person is worth serving, and some dirty work is often needed, even if it is not listed on the job description. Pseudoprofessionals have an image to maintain. Liberated people, on the other hand, see that the professional image may end up maintaining and even constraining us. If we allow our work to define us totally, we literally lose ourselves in it without finding ourselves.

If we think politically and in a global context, again each image can instruct us. On one hand, given the disparity between the rich and the poor in the world, we are warned that the haves may need to have less if the have-nots are to have enough. People with no stomach for self-denial will never respond to such a demand or entreaty except "under the gun." If power is going to be shared with those who have been denied it—developing nations, blacks, Hispanics, women, Native Americans, the poor, those who have had a corner on power need to learn self-denial.

On the other hand, if others are to enjoy the possibility of seeking personal and group liberation instead of merely scratching for survival, as most members of the human race do, it would be better if those who "have it good" sought to assure that possibility for others instead of coveting it for themselves. If schools, corporations, governments, and other institutions leave people no room for self-fulfillment, persons will be only cogs in the machinery of the organization. They will be victims rather than beneficiaries of our vaunted ideologies.

The servant and the liberated person need each other, but the answer to the gap that often opens between them must be more radical than mere mutual correction and edification can provide. Kierkegaard gives us the clue in his analysis of despair, "the sickness unto death." The opposite of despair is faith in God. Faith trusts and, in the security of that trust, can love others. It takes faith to believe that losing ourselves could mean finding ourselves. It takes faith to believe that we are affirmed even when we are not busy affirming ourselves. It takes faith to love at the risk of being hurt. It takes faith to believe that God wills abundant life for all the creation.

In William Golding's *Free Fall,* a novel set during World War II, Samuel Mountjoy's malaise is diagnosed by one of his German captors, Dr. Halde, a psychiatrist: "There is no health in you, Mr. Mountjoy. You do not believe in anything enough to suffer for it or be glad. There is no point at which something has knocked on your door and taken possession of you. You possess yourself. . . . Oh yes, you are capable of a certain degree of friendship and a certain degree of love, but nothing to mark you out from the ants or the sparrows."[39] A life that would distinguish us from the ants and the come to terms with each other as people who have a claim on the necessities of life. We cannot simply focus on our personal well-being and see others as essential contributors to our abundant life; we have to reckon with the presence of the other and with the bread that both comes between us and can unite us. If a health-care provider and a patient or a lawyer and a client see each other as companions, they are acknowledging that they are connected by a problem that has led one to seek the help of the other but that does not make one the superior of the other. They have a bond in which they need each other if what they hold in common is to be managed satisfactorily. In a sense, even an enemy is a companion in that we have a world in common, and both our claims on its resources must be recognized. Companion carries a sense of urgency and inescapability that friendship may not.

Friendship, too, is suggestive.[41] Friends are free to lead their own lives without always having to answer to each other, yet they are tied closely together. The strings attached to friendship can be even stronger than the ties of blood or the bonds of marriage, and good marriages are close friendships. True friendship both frees and obliges. Friends share a common vision of things that really matter, yet they value each others' differences. Friends trust each other; the worst sin is betrayal. Friendship is willing to include strangers; it is not jealous or possessive. In friendship, the feeling is mutual. In friendship, all care is intensive care. In friendship, all studies are longitudinal. Friendship is covenantal; it lasts. Jesus told his disciples that he was calling them servants no longer; instead he would call them friends (John 15:15).

Like all images or metaphors, companion and friend have their limits. We cannot be friends with everyone about whom we should be concerned. Institutional obligations are diluted if we feel obligated only to individual companions and friends. We are not just half a person when not with a friend or companion.

Images of Others

Images of ourselves imply images of others; in fact, images of others may precede our self-images. Experiences of others as aggressors may trigger victim reactions in us. Conversely, our self-images do things to others. If we tend to be parental in our relationships, we may keep others in a childlike relationship to us, or at least we may make the attempt. If we see ourselves primarily as servants, we may find ourselves at loose ends without someone to serve.

What is our image of otherness in general? Do we always stereotype those who are different from us to keep them at arm's length and avoid letting them affect us? If our images of others fuel our

sparrows demands a commitment of faith. Such a commitm
volves both suffering and being glad, both leaving self behi
having life in all its fullness.

Both the servant and the liberated person are good images.
who value biblical authority will find it impossible to ignore
to be a servant people, and we still praise politicians by callin
public servants and corporations by saying that they should
serve the customer. Our chariness about subservience a
abuses of the servant image should not be allowed to depriv
its power. Likewise, a people who worship a liberating G
education as a liberating experience, and consider politica
nomic, religious, and psychological freedom as essential to
well-being should not allow abuses of the liberation image to
of its promise.

A third image escapes some of the problems to which the
two can lead; it is the image of the companion or the friend. 1
Ogletree, in *Hospitality to the Stranger,* has offered a cogent
tive to the tendency in Western ethics to make "the other"
tant because of the essential role that "other" plays in th
integration and self-actualization of the individual who is see
be a centered self. Ogletree insists that the other's initiative
beginning of moral experience, and that the encounter wi
other disrupts my world by requiring some response to anoth
ter of action. The opposite error, however, is to put the self
at the service of the other to the extent that I forswear all ri
my own as claims on the other.[40] The danger then is that ther
empowered self to act morally in response to the other. Og
then, is addressing the dangers in both the image of the serva
that of the liberated person.

Carol Gilligan, as we have already seen, also advances a corr
both to the selfishness that acknowledges no other's claim and
loss of selfhood that puts a person always at others' disposal
vice. Her ethic of care focuses on webs of relationship and in
pendency in which both a person's needs and well-being and o
needs and well-being have a rightful claim to attention and con
ation.

Both *friend* and *companion* define the self as related to
without subjugating one person to another. Both suggest mut
and shared responsibility. *Companion* literally means a sharer
same bread. Sharing food with a person has long indicated clos
and intimacy, and communion around and through a common
carries deep, sacred meaning in many religious communities. N
theless, we should begin our appreciation of the companion ima
an even more basic level. The "bread" to be shared with the
includes not only food but all the world's resources. We ha

fears of those who are different, we shall always practice a morality of protection rather than a morality of openness or hospitality. We shall never go out without our umbrellas and sunscreen to shield us from exposure to the glare of "the other."

The most utterly "other" is, of course, the enemy, and Sam Keen has filled a book with the verbal and pictorial images we project of the enemy.[42] The enemy is variously depicted as the stranger, the aggressor, the faceless power, the enemy of God, the barbarian, the criminal, the torturer, the rapist, the beast, the reptile, the insect, the germ, death, and occasionally the worthy opponent. As the quotation from Keen that heads this chapter indicates, the hostile imagination kills before the weapons do. George Kennan, a long-time realist in foreign affairs who has served our country as ambassador to the Soviet Union, wrote these words in 1981 about the Soviet leaders: "If we insist on demonizing these Soviet leaders—on viewing them as total and incorrigible enemies, consumed only with their own fear or hatred of us and dedicated to nothing other than our destruction—that, in the end, is the way we shall assuredly have them, if for no other reason than that our view of them allows for nothing else, either for us or for them."[43]

Our images of people of other races, other religions, other social classes, other nationalities, and other ethnic groups also reflect our fears of the other, our desire to feel superior to the other, and our hostility toward the other. If we accentuate the differences, we shall feel less identified with "them," less apt to learn from them, and less responsible to and for them.

Our images of the other sex may spell the difference between a morality of exploitation and a morality of mutuality. Women have long and often been regarded as sex objects, as cheap labor, and as childbearers.[44] They have been seen as goddesses and as seductresses, as witches who know too much and as irrational bundles of emotions who know too little. No wonder a major effort in the women's liberation movement has been to generate different metaphors for women and to recover positive features in others (such as witch or Amazon). Emily Culpepper points out the potency of Amazon as "metaphoric identity" because it is a nonvictim identity that empowers resistance to oppression, a strength-validating identity that counters "the weaker sex," and a women-bonding identity that affirms women loving women.[45]

In recent years, men have gotten a taste of being looked at as "hunks," animals, oppressors, and machines. The point is not to imply that men have just as rough a time as women; they do not. The point is that our images of members of the opposite sex carry great moral freight. They may invite exploitation and treatment as an object, or they may open the way for greater sensitivity and mutuality.

Images of Nature

Men's images of women and of the natural world are often parallel. Wendell Berry charges that contemporary Americans tend to view nature as a machine that produces things we want, just as women are viewed as baby-makers. Both are considered to be there for man's use, at his disposal.[46]

The machine image has superseded an older image of nature as the enemy, since the enemy has supposedly been conquered. If science and technology have delivered us from cringing before the power of nature, we can now make it our slave. The hostile environment is now the docile environment.

Another venerable image is that of nature as mother or mystical creative power. Nature is viewed with awe but not regarded as a perennially hostile force. This antithesis of the machine metaphor highlights human indebtedness to nature. Nature should be served rather than be servant. We belong to it; it bats last. Our attitude should be one of awe and care. If a sparrow falls, it had better not be because we shot it; if a species perishes, it had better not be because we hastened its demise. We "wait on" nature.

If the machine metaphor leads to a morality of exploitation and the mystical mother metaphor leads to a morality of acquiescence, there is another metaphor that leads to an ethic of what Wendell Berry calls "husbandry." Berry uses this metaphor to imagine human relations with each other, with nature, and with God. His version of at-one-ment posits a partnership between humans and the natural environment.[47] Nature is mate or companion or friend. In Berry's novel *The Memory of Old Jack*, Jack Beechum has a partnership or a companionship with the land. He is married to it. In their covenantal relationship, which stands in sharp contrast to his failed marriage to Ruth, he and the land give to each other and receive from each other. A deep sense of interdependence replaces worship; respect supersedes abject acquiescence. Both nature and farmer are initiators and receivers before the activity and passivity of the other. Neither is utterly yielding, and neither is wholly assertive.[48]

In our interactions with nature, we count too, but the effects of our actions on nature cannot be discounted. As Berry asserts, in the web of the earth's ecology,

> [Y]ou can't do one thing; each event invariably compounds itself in others. Order ramifies in order; disorder ramifies in disorder. And so great is the magnitude of the order of Creation that no one ever understands the ultimate cause or foresees the ultimate consequences of any act. The human meaning of this is that we are not, have never been, can never be, alone.[49]

Images of God

Although Karl Barth's early designations of God as the "Wholly Other" have been deservedly criticized, even by Barth himself, God is in a way the ultimate Other with which or with whom we must deal. Our images or metaphors for this Other make a powerful moral difference. Seeing God as a warrior king or a bringer of peace (the Hebrews did both in their scripture) lends legitimacy to very diverse undertakings. Regarding God as the strong and dependable rock issues in a response different from one stimulated by an image of God as a capricious trickster. To use Alfred North Whitehead's threesome, the responses vary greatly for believers in God the void, God the enemy, and God the companion ("the fellow sufferer who understands").[50] Ascribing ultimacy to a plurality of chaotic powers or of conjugate pairs has different ethical repercussions from trusting God as a loving parent or an empowering spirit. Discovering that biblical literature uses metaphors for God as a woman giving birth (Isa. 42:14) and nursing (Isa. 49:14–15), as a midwife (Ps. 22:9–10; Isa. 66:9), as a mother hen (Matt. 23:37; Luke 13:34), as a mother eagle (Deut. 32:11–12), and as a mother bear (Hos. 13:8) as well as a father, a shepherd, and a king can be a generative experience for the moral life.

Nelle Morton concludes in *The Journey Is Home* that God the Father has lost whatever metaphoric power it might once have had because of its associations with male domination,[51] and Sallie McFague laments that the father metaphor became the model. God the Father has dominated the theological imagination of Judaism and Christianity. In *Models of God,* McFague explores some different models of God as mother, lover, and friend. Each of these has implications for a particular kind of love, and they lead respectively to ethics of justice, caring, and companionship. For Morton, even the word *God* carried too much negative freight; meeting the Goddess was a transforming experience that put her in touch with the power of the images of God the Mother, woman God, sister God, and lover God. As Carter Heyward observes in reviewing the book, "Most notably for Morton, the Goddess is *not* merely another face of God. She is the antithesis of everything that the patriarchal deity has come to symbolize."[52] The Goddess is with people, not above them; in fact, for some writers, the Goddess is a name for women's power, solidarity, and connectedness to nature. The bottom line is that traditional images of God have led to moralities of enforcement and enfeeblement rather than empowerment for women. Power has been imagined as something some people have over other people instead of something to be shared and to be encouraged in others so that it can be shared. As process theology has urged, power understood as control must give way to power understood as persuasion, beginning at the top (or the bottom) with God or Goddess.

In *Household of Freedom*, Letty Russell recovers the biblical metaphor for God as the housekeeper. Like the woman in Jesus' parable (Luke 15) searching her house, God is looking for the lost people of the world and rejoicing to find them. The household of God knows no outsiders and no outcasts. All can be one in the Spirit. Says Russell, "This is powerful God-talk, which may provide us with language and metaphor equipped for the building up *(oikodome)* of the household of freedom."[53]

The moral freight of our images of God is often obvious, but people's skill at deriving opposite implications from images is scary. Images of God as father, husband, and king have given some fathers, husbands, and kings leave to think of themselves as acting in the place of God and as entitled to the obedience owed to God. On the other hand, such images can prompt humble acknowledgments that fathers, husbands, and rulers stand under divine authority and correction and in constant need of education by divine love, fidelity, and wisdom.

How Models Matter

Models are both extrapolations of metaphors and extractions from myths. In both respects, they risk misrepresentation of their origins for the sake of increasing clarity and spelling out implications. We have already considered some of the liabilities that can accompany what McFague calls the transformation of a metaphor to a model. What was once recognized as one of many ways to see something becomes established as capturing the whole truth. People then tend to forget that metaphors liken something to something else but still assume an unlikeness too. It is inevitable and even necessary that we develop models to enhance understanding and draw contrasts, but we should discard the chisels we use to engrave them in stone.

Without organizing a parade of models, I suggest a pair of contrasts to illustrate the moral momentum of models: the contrast between the market model and the public health model in providing health care and the contrast between the biomedical, scientific model and the biopsychosocial model in "imagining" illness and health.

When the market model prevails, the provider of health care is like the baker of bread.[54] The baker has acquired a skill and now provides something the public wants. The baker is free to do business or not to do business with people depending on their ability to pay and the baker's willingness to prepare the bread. Economic gain is what drives the system. The public health model starts with the needs of the community. It assumes that all the members of the community should enjoy good health and have health care and plots strategies to do the best possible job of meeting those needs with the skills and resources available.[55]

The first model makes defending the individual rights of the baker the primary consideration; the second makes meeting the needs of the community the top priority. Arguments over public policy often root in opposing models, with their roots in opposing metaphors and myths (the subject of the next chapter). More basic than the conflict between the principles of individual liberty and social justice is a disagreement over the kind of activity the provision of health care is. Is it like being in the bread business or being sure everyone in the family gets food? Is health care like a desirable item for which we shop or a necessity of life that no one should be denied? There is truth in both models, and problems multiply when one model is pursued so uncritically that its limited vision is ignored. Today the British system, which has been based on the community-health model, is looking at the use of market incentives within the system to encourage greater efficiency. The American system, which has been based on the market model, is recognizing the need for better ways to meet the health-care needs of thirty-seven million Americans who have no health insurance.

The traditional biomedical, scientific model for approaching health problems focuses on disease, which is caused by a biochemical or structural lesion. A disease is an entity that attacks a person, and medical interventions are search-and-destroy operations in the human body or restorations of chemical or structural balances in the brain. The biopsychosocial model as articulated by George Engel[56] places the person in an ecosystem that reaches inward to the nervous system, organs and organ systems, tissue, cells, organelles, and molecules but also reaches outward to family members, doctors, friends, and other interpersonal relations, and that reaches also the nuclear and extended family, the community, the sub-culture or culture, the society or nation, and the biosphere.

At the University of Louisville Medical School, Dr. Gabriel Smilkstein has introduced "humble rounds" to go along with the traditional "grand rounds." In grand rounds, the biomedical model comes to focus on the smallest possible piece of the patient where the disease in located, and doctors discuss the most effective intervention to solve the problem. The danger is that the patient as a person may be overlooked. In humble rounds, the view of the patient is expanded to bring in psychosocial considerations in the setting of an illness, not just a disease. As the complexity grows, the likelihood of a simple fix shrinks; but the person stays in full view. The danger here could be that the urgency of unleashing the best skill and technology on the disease could be mitigated by attention to a long list of ailments. Both models have value, but the "humble rounds" model has been sadly neglected in contemporary Western medical training and practice.

These contrasting models should demonstrate that ethical concern should not begin with decisions about which actions to take. Ethics begins with differing visions of what is going on, and our models filter those interpretations.

Measuring Metaphors, Images, and Models

The metaphors, images, and models that figure prominently in the social worlds we inhabit and the imaginative filters through which we view them are a mixed bag. I have dropped more than hints that some are better than others; yet there is not some transcendent sphere above all metaphors, images, and models where we can position ourselves to pass objective judgment on their relative merits and demerits. We inevitably use some metaphors, images, and models to criticize others, and we have made the first important step if we assume that not one of them is beyond criticism. Metaphoric fundamentalism is not the answer even when the metaphors are the cream of the crop. We also inevitably make our assessments from within a worldview, an outlook that is expressed in narrative form through myth and story, the subjects of the next chapter.

What questions should we ask of these imaginative frames? The following questions deserve at least a place on our list. Does the image give integrity to people and their several spheres of activity, their plural roles, and their various relationships, or does it squeeze them into a constricted profile that is only appropriate to a small sample of people's activities and worsens a fragmented self-image? What attitudes and actions does the image of the other (including the outsider, the enemy, and the natural world) justify or encourage? What consequences will our frames and filters bring about? What view of people's relatedness or self-containment and of their potential for good and evil do they imply? Do they suggest a world neatly divided between the good people in the white hats and the bad people in the black ones?

Summary

The questions we use to assess metaphors, images, and models finally push to questions about the stories, myths, and worldviews that underlie them. Metaphors may break into stories, as Malamud's Cohn put it, but on the flip side, stories and myths spawn metaphors and models. Therefore our consideration of imaginative contexts moves in the next chapter to stories, myths, and worldviews.

All of these aspects of the universe of language that we inhabit and that indwells us are creations of the human imagination. They are contexts of ethics because they are part of our social world. They are points of view and also points of contact. They are both because we never see and touch our world naked. We always see it clothed in the apparel with which our metaphors, images, models, myths, and worldviews dress it. Like the institutions we inhabit, these imaginative contexts are both filters of our perceptions and settings of our moral choices.

EVERYBODY HAS A CHOICE. YOU WOULDNT HAVE TO BE POOR IF YOU DIDN'T **WANT** TO BE.

ITS A FREE COUNTRY, YOU WOULDN'T HAVE TO BE UNEMPLOYI IF YOU DIDN'T WANT TO BE

THIS IS THE LAND OF OPPORTUNITY YOU WOULDN'T HAVE TO BE BADLY EDU-CATED IF YOU DIDN'T **WANT** TO BE

EVERY BOY CAN BE PRES-IDENT. YOU WOULDNT HAVE TO BE AN ADDICT IF YOU DIDNT **WANT** TO BE.

ALL IT TAKES IS INITIATIVE YOU WOULDNT HAVE TO TURN TO CRIME IF YOU DIDN'T **WANT** IT TO BE.

EVERYBODY HAS A CHOICE I WOULDN'T HAVE TO BE DEAD IF I DIDN'T **WANT** TO BE

5
Imaginative Contexts:
Stories, Myths, and Worldviews

Peters and Waterman can convince a reader that corporations are known and know themselves by the stories they tell, and Robert Reich is equally convincing in saying that Americans know themselves by the parables, morality tales, and myths they tell. "Much," he writes, "is made of the American political distinctiveness of a Constitution inspired by theory rather than by tradition. But there is a subtler yet equally profound *cultural* distinctiveness as well, a national sense of identity rooted not in history but in self-told mythology." When we debate issues, our myth-based morality tales are always in the background because "the basic contours of our mythology organize the way we think about issues; they bound the field of argument."[1] American political culture is every bit as storied and mythic as corporate cultures are, if not more so.

Americans are not unusual in their reliance on values articulated in story and myth to identify themselves. The definition of a community's identity through stories and myths that provide a common vision and locate a group of people against a larger horizon of meaning is a human trait, not an American peculiarity. As Robert Reich sees it, "Cultural myths are no more 'truth' than an architect's sketches are buildings. Their function is to explain events and guide decisions."[2] If his statement means that our myths do not exhaust the truth or fully capture reality, it is apt. If people take it to mean that myths never tell the truth about human existence, they are mistaken.

Robert Bellah asserts, "Myth does not attempt to describe reality; that is the job of science. Myth seeks rather to transfigure reality so that it provides moral and spiritual meanings to individuals and societies."[3] But even science is not mythless; it has its interpretative filters that determine what counts for truth and what is worth knowing. The point is that the human imagination provides contexts for us that we may label myths or worldviews or ideologies, if that last term is not confined to mere rationalizations of the conditions that serve our economic interests. Ideologies may be stated in proposition, but myths are narrative contexts of a community's or a society's existence. Both myths and ideologies are worldviews.

Roger Shinn distinguishes between Ideology A and Ideology B. Ideology A refers to a false consciousness that Karl Marx and Karl Mannheim designate as ideology. This brand of ideology results from a person's or group's desire to justify a privileged position by buttressing it with a system of economic, political, or religious thought. It is a *"distortion of reality,"* and it both victimizes other people and digs the grave of the perpetrators. Ideology B refers to *"a set of conceptions or a picture of society and the world that helps to guide action."* [4] In this sense, having an ideology is a necessity for us to function, not a mere buttress of the bourgeoisie.

Our discussion of metaphor and image and model could not stop until it reached story and myth, the natural habitat of metaphor. Now our discussion of story and myth will take us inexorably to worldview and faith or religion. Whatever imaginative filter or frame of reference places people in some context of meaning that encompasses all of life is their religion, whether there are any gods in the picture or not.

Mythic Conflicts in American Society

Numerous tensions and conflicts in our society's life can be traced to mythic roots. For centuries sex roles were dictated in large measure by myths about the roles of men and women, which could be stated in ideological capsule form as "A woman's place is in the home." By implication, a man's place was in the public realm, and a woman's place was not the executive suite, the pulpit, the judicial bench, or the surgeon's arena. Those myths have taken a vigorous and well-deserved beating in our time. A new mythic capsule began to appear on T-shirts: A WOMAN'S PLACE IS IN THE HOUSE—AND THE SENATE. This change in our myths has meant a reassessment of our marriages, a re-vision of vocational horizons, and a re-view of what it means to be a man as well as what it means to be a woman.

Those who discerned the roots of women's subordination and exploitation knew all along that demanding the vote or admission to male-dominated professional enclaves or equal pay for equal work or pregnancy leaves was important but that it did not go deeply enough. As we saw in the previous chapter, new images for men and women are essential if they are to foresee different lives for themselves and for one another. Even different images of God are necessary if women are to claim fully their birthright. We needed to tell better stories about ourselves, either by reinterpreting and revising old ones or by discovering new ones. Children's literature had to be reexamined for its sexist assumptions. When the Moral Majority started scanning school textbooks for pictures, stories, and theories that undermined traditional sex roles, they knew what they were doing. Their assumptions about a lot of things are at stake in the stories the young are taught to tell about themselves.

As part of the myth shift, the Bible has been "depatriarchalized,"as Phyllis Trible puts it.[5] For instance, the Mary myth that a male-dominated church had used to elevate the ideal of motherhood and denigrate sexuality could also be rediscovered as a liberating force. The Mary of the Magnificat nurtured not only Jesus but sisters and brothers of future generations who would help to "put down the mighty from their thrones" and exalt those of "low degree" (Luke 1:52). Other conscientious objectors to the old myths have been midwives for the birth or recovery of different myths centered on the Goddess or values in ancient witchcraft that were denigrated by a male religious establishment. Myths can be mightier than constitutional amendments, although it usually takes political and economic pressure, as well as confrontation by a compelling alternative myth, to make those who are served well by the status quo see the error of the conventional myths.

Such African-American writers as Toni Morrison and Alice Walker have not only told the stories of their people's suffering but have also led the search for a usable past. *Song of Solomon*, by Morrison, and *The Color Purple*, by Walker, put the reader in touch with African roots, including myths, and repudiate white people's definitions of African-Americans. Through song and through story, people threatened with cultural extinction keep their bearings as well as bear their keeping. Out of the stories of their forebears and out of their own interpretation of the dominant culture's religion came a liberation ethic to see them through the wilderness and take them to the promised land. In the process, racial myths that had lent legitimacy to slavery, apartheid, and discrimination were challenged and repudiated, although minority views such as those held by the Ku Klux Klan and white supremacists still persist.

Conflicting myths about our relationship to nature have also been locked in struggle in our society. The images of nature that we treated earlier are rooted in worldviews and myths. When Ronald Reagan said, while governor of California, "If you have seen one redwood, you have seen them all," he was articulating the view that nature is here to be used as we see fit for our immediate ends. The bumper sticker that reads NATURE BATS LAST insists that we realize our dependence on the environment and our accountability for poor stewardship of it.

In his much-debated article "The Historical Roots of Our Ecologic Crisis,"[6] Lynn White, Jr., was too hard on the biblical tradition, but he was right about the importance of the Hebrew myths of creation for Western culture's relation to nature. The charge to "fill the earth and subdue it and have dominion" (Gen. 1:28) was more than a permission; it was a vocation to explore and understand nature. And it combined with a Greek view of nature to open the door to a later notion, very different from the Hebrew stewardship of nature, that humanity could live off nature rather than with it. The story of creation in Genesis 2 balances the vocation of dominion with the charge to till and keep the Garden of Eden; but the attitude still contrasts with the more acquiescent relationship of humankind to nature that we find among Native Americans and in Eastern religions. White recognized that people cannot just spawn new myths whenever they feel like doing it and that a Buddhist myth of human relation to nature is not apt to take the West by storm. He suggested instead "the search for a usable past," to borrow Henry Steele Commager's title,[7] in the Christian tradition and nominated Francis of Assisi as the patron saint of ecologists.

Another mythic clash in our culture can be briefed as a conflict between "bigger is better" and "small is beautiful."[8] The myth of inevitable progress that held much of the West in its spell in the late nineteenth and early twentieth centuries, and still lives in many a heart, lies behind the widespread push for more of everything. When an energy crisis alerted us to the rapid depletion of nonrenewable resources and some people began talking about "conservation barrels of oil" (saving one is as good as discovering one), many voices added approving responses to the Texas executive's indignant retort, "This country did not conserve its way to greatness." We had always assumed that growth could go on forever and that growth would involve more energy use and that everyone would benefit from more growth.[9] The sky was the limit. Unchallenged, the growth metaphor was worshipfully followed. The problem was, as Richard Grossman captures it, "Quality has no measure in the language of growth and inequality has no column."[10]

Then came E. F. Schumacher's talk of "appropriate technology" and "Buddhist economics" and "living with limits." The Club of Rome's extrapolations in *The Limits to Growth* about the rapidity with which we would start running out of things proved to be false;[11] the energy crisis proved to be temporary, and people appropriately contended that bigger may be better for the general welfare in some cases. Still the conventional wisdom that said "the sky is the limit" had come under suspicion, and it will probably never again enjoy the unchallenged reign that it once did.

Conflicting views of the United States' role in the world are also mythic clashes. Ever since John Winthrop described us as "the city set on a hill," we have liked to think of ourselves as a chosen people, a new Israel, a people with a manifest destiny. Chauvinistic versions of our civil religion substituted national self-justification for the national self-criticism that drew on the "religion" of the Constitution and the Declaration of Independence to free slaves, enfranchise women, and expand civil rights. Our nation developed what Arthur Schlesinger, Jr., has called a "global messianism."[12] Captain America could right the world's wrongs and lead the backward peoples to the light.

The Vietnam War dealt a near-fatal blow to this myth. Finding that we had to destroy villages in order to "save" them, that we were often unable to tell the fighting force of the enemy from civilians, that we could not jerk the situation into a shape we desired, and that watching our people and the Vietnamese die in droves on the evening news was hard on the digestion, we experienced widespread disillusionment. The process of responding to the traumas of the returning veterans, receiving large numbers of Vietnamese refugees, and recovering or discovering a better myth to inform our international relations has been long and painful.[13]

A story from the war that lacks the grisly horror of the My Lai massacre but still illustrates the mythic impasse of the war tells about the WHAM project[14] (WHAM stood for "win the hearts and minds"). One of its campaigns was an attack (note the metaphor) on tooth decay among Vietnamese children. Helicopters carrying dentists and their assistants descended on villages. A village would be surrounded. The men were taken away for interrogation. The rest of the people were herded together to hear American band music and later to see a propaganda film. Using candy and other gifts, the well-intentioned strangers enticed children and took them temporarily from bemused parents for treatment. They prodded teeth with strange-looking instruments and in some instances pulled them. Men of military age were taken away to serve in the South Vietnamese army. Children from a quiet, subdued Buddhist culture were encouraged by the Americans to be loud and even unruly. Blind and deaf to the myths and stories of the "invaded" people, the heart-winners wondered why filling cavities and clearing plaque did not fill the gulf between "them" and "us." Meanwhile the Vietnamese worried that the Vietcong would blame them for the Americans' presence. In a similar way, our effort there overlooked centuries of Vietnamese experience and a mythic context that set a mere decade of the present struggle in a larger story of struggle against domination by Chinese and French for generations.

The division of the nation over Vietnam was deeply damaging to national identity and self-respect. The Reagan victories and popularity reflect the warm welcome we accord someone who will tell us that the myths we have long held dear still make sense. A lot of people were tired of "blame America." The "chosen people" rhetoric flourished again, and efforts to refurbish a Christian image of the nation swelled with the growth of the religious right's support for school prayer, reversal of legalized abortion, and military opposition to third world governments tainted with Marxism. The invasion of Grenada and the bombing of Libya put spring in some steps, and the Contras of Nicaragua were baptized as "freedom fighters" and spiritual heirs of our Founding Fathers despite their terrorism and their unpopularity with most of the Nicaraguan people.

In debates over a nuclear freeze, the Intermediate-range Nuclear Forces (INF) treaty, and the Strategic Defense Initiative ("Star Wars"), settling for "sufficiency" or even "parity" in nuclear arms has been hard to stomach for those who find anything short of nuclear superiority incompatible with our reigning national myth. Somewhere in the woodwork still lurk beliefs that nuclear wars have winners, that we can win one, and that we owe it to the survival of our way of life to gear our policies toward victory in a nuclear war. First strikes and destabilizing steps then become "live" options, and our suspicions blind us to the possibility that we and the Soviets share a great overlap of self-interest in avoiding a nuclear exchange or even a continuing nuclear arms buildup. Acting on the basis of worst-case scenarios and assumptions that Gorbachev's overtures to de-escalate the arms race must be tricks runs the great risk of provoking the very actions we fear.

In American attitudes toward nuclear war, our national myth about our place in the world sometimes combines with mythic outlooks toward history's end that are found in certain religious traditions. Ira Chernus has argued convincingly in *Dr. Strangegod: On the Symbolic Meaning of Nuclear Weapons*[15] that some mythologies about nuclear war have served to keep people from facing what a nuclear war would be like. If our policy decisions are to be well informed, we need to be telling each other better stories about nuclear war. Chernus believes that three ancient and recurring religious myths are compromising our ability to think realistically.

One is the myth of the heroic survivors. Either as an instance of a repeating cycle of death and rebirth or as the apocalyptic final judgment on an evil world, a nuclear war would enable the heroes, having gone through the ordeal of testing, to make a fresh start. Chernus cites the U.S. senator who said that, if there has to be a new Adam and Eve, he wants them to be Americans. Whether a technological Lone Ranger or some "wise man" or our own faithfulness saves us, we can take comfort in being among those who will make a fresh start. This myth encourages us to believe (1) that there will be survivors, (2) that we will be among them, and (3) that we would want to be among them in the grim and chaotic world that remained.

The myth of total extinction is Chernus's second culprit. This myth of the "big whoosh" puts us squarely under the mushroom cloud. If the first myth gains a certain transcendence by positing survivors, this one neutralizes the threat by envisioning a quick and painless death for everyone. This final, explosive plunge into cosmic unity offers "transcendence through annihilation."[16] The problem is that most Americans would survive the initial blasts and even half of us might "live" through the first month to "enjoy" the rampant disease, the abnormal behavior, the bitter conflicts, and the repressive controls that would come in the war's wake.

Then there is the myth of fate or destiny. We are powerless to forestall whatever is in the cards. What makes this response religious in company with the other two is that we are awed and worshipful before an awesome, controlling power. These three options are ways of coming to terms with that power.

Although Chernus debunks these myths for shielding us from the realities of what a nuclear war would involve and absolving us of responsibility, he contends that the scientific and technological literature about nuclear war is itself mythological. It depersonalizes the phenomenon with all the facts and figures and again screens us from the personal import of it all. Still, he does not advocate that we attempt to shed all myth (demythologize). It could be self-defeating even if it were possible. "[I]t is questionable whether the human mind can deal with the complexity and enormity of the chaos of nuclear war on an empirical demythologized level." Since it is extremely difficult and probably impossible to create new myths intentionally, Chernus attempts to "remythologize" by elevating the myth of the existential antihero. This figure must wander the earth in a state between life and death, "condemned to make decisions in a situation where no truly heroic action is possible."[17] This is a better myth because it insists that we must decide and that our decisions are of great moment, and it does not deny how high the stakes are.

G. Simon Harak, like Chernus a religion professor, has also provided a forceful argument for the role of myth in our thinking about the nuclear arms race. While Chernus looks to the history of religions for his myths, Harak draws on America's civil religion in analyzing "the soteriology [doctrine of salvation] of SDI [the Strategic Defense Initiative, or Star Wars]."[18] President Reagan's 1983 proposal for a defensive umbrella against the missiles of our enemies has been effectively attacked because it will put an umbrella only over our missile sites at best, because its cost is astronomical, and because it would destabilize the arms race if successful, yet it is a proposal that has been hard to kill. There are mythic reasons for its hardiness;

they reside in the religious symbol system of our nation, which Robert Bellah and others have dubbed the American civil religion.

In the Reagan vision, the very scientific community that created the sinful nuclear power (at government expense, he might have added) can now be the smiths of our salvation by turning these offensive possibilities to a pure, defensive use. The earlier ritual of creating the bomb, and in the end making us vulnerable from the sky as well, can now be repeated to provide us with the protection against threats from above that our oceans provide from threats to our shores. Once again we would be a sanctuary, a "virgin" land protected from the evil world's aggression, as we saw ourselves in our nation's beginnings. SDI would put us back in control of our destiny again. We could turn the clock back to the time before Hiroshima, or at least to the time when only we had the bomb, or at the very least to a sure protection of our launching capability. If people ask why the defensive Star Wars weaponry could not be turned to offensive use, they are told that the Russians know that we would never strike first.

The salvation offered by SDI lends support to a holy-crusade mentality about a possible nuclear war. Because we would be using SDI to preserve the free world, our efforts would receive what John Howard Yoder calls "transcendent validation."[19] Our national shift from counter-value targeting (against population centers) to counter-force targeting (against missile silos) has already made first strikes attractive. We would knock out their missiles before they could knock ours out. Combine the counter-force strategy with SDI, and we have the ingredients for a holy war as the means of preempting evil while shielded from assaults on our weapons. Because SDI as protection has a purity that the bomb did not, it becomes a guarantor of our regained purity as the adversary of evil in the world. We do not have to seek the path of negotiation because we would have regained our old invulnerability. Thus as long as we operate with our myth about American purity, we shall be loath to relinquish the vain hope SDI claims to offer.

Our examples of myths' influence on morality and public policy have underlined the importance of these imaginative contexts of ethics, but we have not yet been specific about the import of myth for the ethics of professionals in particular. Two penetrating analyses of our nation's political culture will assist toward that end: *Tales of a New America*, by Robert B. Reich, and *Habits of the Heart*, by Robert Bellah and colleagues.

Political Culture as Professional Context

We already know that Reich recognizes the permeation of political culture by mythology, that "indispensable conceptual shorthand, the means by which we comprehend, come to terms with, and talk about complicated social realities." Our myths he sees as "almost unconscious," permeating our metaphors and allusions, while morality tales, which are based in our myths, are told in order to teach lessons.[20] At least four morality tales permeate our particular national culture, according to Reich: the Mob at the Gates, the Triumphant Individual, the Benevolent Community, and the Rot at the Top. Each of these "core parables" (a use of the term that biblical scholars would dispute) has been a powerful influence in our public life; each has both conservative and liberal versions; and each must assume new versions and provide new visions to keep pace with a changed world that has challenged the adequacy of the old versions. Both liberal and conservative versions of each of them pits "us" against "them" in ways that will not make a "new America" possible.

The Mob at the Gates can be the Soviets, the immigrants, the Japanese, the poor who do not pull their weight, third world countries, our allies, drug traffickers, or terrorists. Each of them in some way seems to pose a threat to our political or economic well-being. Believing that liberals followed the way of appeasing, placating, and coddling for too long, conservatives have accentuated the way of discipline, defiance, and toughness. But the "us" against "them" polarity does not describe today's world adequately.

The Japanese-American corporation blurs definition of our economic aim as a victory in competition for either one nation or the other. The drug problem is as much our problem as it is that of the drug-exporting nations. In the new global economy, we cannot feign self-sufficiency and dominance. We need imports from the third world. When a recession hits, we learn that unemployment is not just "their" problem. We have waves of legal and illegal immigrants because of economic conditions in their countries that we often helped create or perpetuate and conditions in our job market that mean some of us want to rely on cheap labor from beyond the gates. We and the Soviets have a mutual stake in avoiding a holocaust. We and they will win or lose together. We can no longer act alone in this highly interdependent world. Getting tough with "them" can become a boomerang that hits "us" harder than it hits "them." In Reich's words, "There is evil abroad in the world to be sure. But there is no mob. And there are no gates."[21]

The way of promise is neither aggression nor appeasement but recognition of mutual self-interest in a global economy. There are still adversaries to be opposed, but we can no longer pretend to be an island of virtuous self-sufficiency any longer. By finding common cause with those we have called "them," both inside and outside our gates, and by learning what we ultimately have to gain from the empowerment of wasted lives, we discover a companionship that is prompted by facing facts and not just by acting out of the goodness of our hearts. The Mob at the Gates is out of date for conservatives and liberals alike.

The conservative story has pictured the potentially triumphant individuals—the entrepreneurs—being held back by the drones in the economy. The traditional liberal answer of using government spending to create demand has also created more inflation and diluted the resources of those who could get the economy moving again. The conservative answer is to discipline "them" by increasing unemployment, and the liberal answer is to create full employment so that "they" will become full participants in the economy and to put constraints on plant closings and layoffs that harm the work force. But the world has changed. Team triumphs and collective entrepreneurship are increasingly the way to productivity and organizational strength. For Reich, "[T]he central problem of economic policy becomes less how to discipline drones or tease the last ounce of genius out of lone entrepreneurs, but rather how to create the kinds of organizations in which people can pool their efforts, insights, and enthusiasms without fear of exploitation."[22]

The key to such organizations is trust, Reich asserts. Professional partnerships and small businesses producing service-intensive goods have shown the way with sharing of responsibilities and shrinking of hierarchy, and now large corporations are seeking ways to create a sense of community that goes beyond alliances of legal contract. It takes trust for owners and workers to make mutual investments in each other. Without trust, gridlock ensues. If workers have moderated their wage demands and then received no future consideration from ownership, they are not apt to make future concessions. If workers share profits or receive stock options, they are more apt to invest their best efforts and ideas in the companies. Owners invest in workers by giving training and experience with new technologies when they believe that workers are making long-term investments of themselves in the company. Suppliers and creditors, too, can make a difference with their investments in a firm. It is not easy for Americans to shift from their traditional tale of the triumphant individual to Japan's loyal teammate, but collective entrepreneurship has promise for whole organizations if they can learn to tell better stories about themselves. It sounds downright covenantal, doesn't it?

The Benevolent Community is also a myth in trouble. As private citizens, Americans are big on helping others, but the Reagan era revealed deep suspicions and disillusionments with welfare programs for "them." The liberal commitment to charity for the poor gave way to surveillance, cutbacks, and imposition of discipline on "them." Our hardiest and biggest welfare programs have been social insurance for all of us, such as Social Security and Medicare. Americans believe people should be responsible for themselves, yet they can imagine being temporarily unemployed, suffering some handicap or costly illness, lacking enough to live on in retirement, or dying and leaving needy dependents behind. They do not identify, however, with the plight of being born poor, and they do not see their children in that predicament.

The Feiffer cartoon at the beginning of this chapter says a pageful about American suspicions of the poor's lack of effort. The liberal claim that the poor suffer from deprivation more than shiftlessness and that they are entitled to a decent standard of living was not a widespread conviction even in the heyday of the War on Poverty. According to Reich, "Even at the height of the Great Society in 1967, fully 42 percent of Americans thought that poverty reflected mostly a 'lack of effort,' and another 39 percent believed that lack of effort had something to do with it. Only 19 percent concluded that poverty was due to 'circumstances beyond the control' of the poor."[23]

During the Great Depression, when a fourth of the work force was unemployed, people did not think of them as a morally flawed subgroup. Poverty was "our" problem, not just "their" problem. Now the perception is different, despite the facts that one of three Americans fell below the poverty line at least once between 1975 and 1985 and that, among the non-elderly poor, two-thirds lived in a family in which someone worked and most received no welfare payments. During that period, half of the poor remained below the poverty line only one or two years, and 20 percent remained perennially mired in urban or rural pockets of poverty.[24] As Reich observes, "[M]ost of the poor are not very different from the rest of us," but the stigma continues. According to Kin Hubbard, who is quoted in Kurt Vonnegut's *Slaughterhouse-Five*, "It ain't no disgrace to be poor, but it might as well be."[25]

Neither the conservative nor the liberal version of the tale will work. We must recover a sense of being in the same boat. Every person in each new generation must be initiated into a "culture of shared responsibility and mutual benefit."[26] Corporations and prepaid legal plans and health plans are pointing the way in making members of groups responsible to each other for keeping costs down while being assured of the benefits of group membership. As matters now stand, the poor are the separated others, the people with no group identification that provides the combination of mutual responsibility and mutual benefit. Solidarity, not charity, is the story we must tell about ourselves. Solidarity acknowledges that we are inextricably bound up with one another in an interdependent society or world; charity elects to help "them" if "we" have love in our hearts. (And if "they" deserve it, some would add.) All our social programs should build in reciprocal responsibility, and our residential arrangements must change to relieve the isolation of the poor. We must come to the realization that including and enabling a new generation not only makes these people self-supporting; what they have to offer ends up benefiting all of us.

The final tale that needs a new twist is the one Reich calls the Rot at the Top. Conservatives have tended to locate the rot in the politically powerful; liberals have been inclined to make the economic elite the heavies. Suspicion of the powerful is a healthy instinct, but our sweeping indictments of either the top dogs of government or the top dogs of the corporations are too simplistic. The fundamental problem is irresponsibility and lack of stewardship. It is imperative for government to assure that economic activity is not working at cross-purposes with the good of all citizens; it is equally imperative that business keep up with the rapid development of the global economy. Reich concludes:

> We will know our mythology of the Rot at the Top is evolving appropriately when we tell fewer stories that sweepingly denounce either the greed of the businessmen or the meddlesomeness of government—the chaos of the markets or the scourge of planning—and when our scorn falls instead on private power that is willfully unmindful of the public interest and public power that neglects the importance of harnessing private initiative.[27]

Reich is on to something important. "Us" against "them" will continue to be our undoing unless we learn to tell stories of solidarity and stewardship, of mutual responsibility and mutual benefit, of mutual trust and mutual triumphs, of converging self-interest and expanding community. Legal contracts will not bring us together. It will take a political culture that is in sync with today's facts of life and that is transmitted through better myths and stories than we have been telling each other.

How can we recover myths that affirm our interdependence? How do we learn to tell better stories about ourselves? Reich seems to believe that a clear-eyed look at the facts of life in today's world will convince us, but our assessments of the "facts" are always shaped by the stories and myths we inhabit. Reich's advocacy for solidarity and interdependence reflects his own mythic location, not just the needs of our time. Our ability to block out contradictions to our settled assumptions is highly developed. Unless a different slant on the old stories or a new myth captures our imaginations, we persist in our perspectives. As Ian Barbour asserts about both scientific and religious patterns of interpretation, it takes promising alternatives to our filters, not simply contradictory data, to convert us.[28]

Reich is probably too optimistic about the likelihood of swelling recognition of the interdependence of our world economy, although he recognizes that the interests of some groups are simply too sharply opposed to be reconciled. What I would not want to concede, however, is his claim: "We will never be able to enlarge the sphere of 'us' to encompass everyone."[29] Even if he is right about the inevitable clash of interests, it makes a powerful difference whether we tell stories that put everyone in the same boat with interdependent futures or we begin from the presumption that certain divisions can never be healed.

Habits of the Heart also addresses the political culture in which Americans function, examines the myth of the Triumphant Individual, and advocates a moral ecology movement that will show us our interdependence. However, it is no mere earlier version of Reich's argument. It deals with individualism as America's myth in more depth and with greater nuance; it addresses the predicament of the professional more directly, and it also points to other resources for the recovery of commitment and community.

The malaise Bellah and his colleagues diagnose in the American ethos is the dominance of radical individualism, to them a cancerous condition that splits private and public life and destroys our ability to talk about the common good. In the American story, radical individualism has been balanced by two forms of individualism that have tied personal identity to community membership. These are the biblical individualism of John Winthrop and the civic individualism of Thomas Jefferson. (Some question the use of the label *individualism* to cover these more communitarian positions, but these authors do elect to do so.) In contemporary America the utilitarian individualism of Benjamin Franklin and the expressive individualism of Walt Whitman have not only gained the upper hand; they also seem to be the only languages we know how to speak. Utilitarian individualism calculates everything in terms of economic and material payoff, and it assumes that everyone's pursuit of economic well-being will result in the best conditions for all, without the need to consider the public good. Expressive individualism measures every relationship and activity for its emotional payoff. Jobs, marriages, family relationships, political affiliations, and religious memberships get good or bad marks according to how they make us feel.

An old friend of mine once attended a church youth-group meeting with a young woman he liked and happened to hit the night when the pastor of that flock was attacking the evils of dancing. My friend listened attentively as the preacher described all the sinful things that went on as people danced and as a result of their dancing. After the program my friend spoke to the leader long enough to tell him, "I just haven't been getting all out of dancing that I ought to be getting out of it." He captured expressive individualism in a nutshell. Its devotees weigh all associations and activities by how much they are getting out of them, and they find it difficult to rate their current marriage over their last one, or their current way of life over another, other than to say that they feel better about it.

Against this profile of our cultural mores, the authors pit a different vision of "a morally coherent life." For the socially unsituated self they would substitute a self who is constituted by membership in communities of memory and hope. True community is inclusive; it celebrates the interdependence of public and private life and the variety of callings of its diverse members. Our current "life-style enclaves" celebrate "the narcissism of similarity."[30] Even marriages and families have increasingly become such enclaves rather than intergenerational institutions.

In community, selves are defined by obligations and commitments, not simply by arbitrary preferences. These selves are located in narratives, in institutional contexts, and in cultural patterns of meaning. Growth is therefore not defined in purely private terms, and participation in politics carries a moral mandate. Community, then, is no contractual exchange; it is a covenantal commitment.

The dominance of radical individualism has brought the prominence of managers and therapists.[31] Both managers and therapists illustrate the rule of utilitarian individualism in public life and expressive individualism in private life. Both take the organization of industrial society for granted and work to bring about efficient functioning within the system. Both are specialists who assist people in combining occupation and life-style in such a way as to produce the accepted ends of economic productivity and personal self-fulfillment. The manager's role is to engineer the parts of the organization to meet the owners' standards of efficiency. The therapist's role is to help people find a psychologically rewarding life, probably in spite of work and in a sphere separated from work by a substantial distance.

In contrast to this professional manager or therapist as a specialist who facilitates smooth functioning within an unquestioned corporate system, the authors advocate the recovery of professions as callings. Today's professionalism lacks content; it seeks better means for uncriticized ends. When a profession is a calling, it carries moral meaning and it creates links between public and private life. An ethic of community responsibility replaces a division of life into sectors, a split that assigns public life to experts and personal freedom to the private domain.

Covenantal Communities as Cultural Models

Where are the communities of memory and hope in which people can recover integrity between private and public life? Where do we discover the myths that teach us human solidarity and interdependence? Where can people learn to regard their professions as callings? Where might we begin to see justice as more than equal opportunity to pursue private happiness, as, instead, fair distribution of society's benefits? Reich sees the need for smaller organizations and communities to teach mutual trust, mutual obligation, and mutual benefit, but his nominees are corporations, professional associations, and pluralistic residential communities (to replace the vanished neighborhoods). He does not mention religious communities as critical shapers of political culture, as pivotal teachers of the stories we tell each other. He also omits educational institutions as settings for "tales of a new America."

The authors of *Habits of the Heart* are not guilty of neglecting religious communities. They regard religious institutions as probably our last and best hope to counteract the ravages of radical individualism. American religion has often reflected the disastrous effects of rampant individualism, just as the rest of our culture does. It often exacerbates the public-private split and reflects the consumerism inherent in shopping for good feelings instead of making long-term commitments to a community of faith, hope, and love. "Sheilaism," as Bellah terms the private faith of one Sheila Larson, is the ultimate example.[32] Still, religious communities at their best set people within a story; span generations, classes, professions, and races; and strengthen both memory and hope.

In the biblical tradition, religious communities at their best are circles of support and givers of intensive and extensive care. Instead of being temporary stops for religious shoppers hunting for low-demand, good-vibration experiences, they should be permanent families of inclusive, attentive, and empowering love. They should be grounded in gratitude and committed to justice and peace for the long haul. The opposite of "life-style enclaves," which share sameness as long as it feels good, they should welcome diversity in the company of those who share a common center of loyalty, a common commandment to love, and a common ground for hope.

Colleges and universities also offer rich resources at their best, but neither book mentions them, perhaps because they mostly reflect merely the myths of our political culture in their most questionable forms. Students are often treated as consumers to be pleased, or as potential triumphant individuals to prevail in the test of academic competition, or as possessors of individual rights with no corresponding obligations, or as parties to a contract in which both sides are careful to discharge their parts of the bargain. In none of these cases is the educational institution a covenantal community in which people are united by common loyalties, bonded by lasting mutual responsibilities to and for each other, and set within a story that provides meaning, memory, and hope. Because students are, by design, only temporarily members of specific academic communities, it may seem impossible to make these communities truly covenantal. It is still possible, however, in an individualistic and contractual society to build such communities of learning.

The contractual model and its underlying individualistic myth have brought some benefits to higher education. An assumed contract tempers institutional tendencies to make grandiose claims in catalogs and admissions literature. It guarantees that minimal expectations are met for students who have the temerity to believe that the professors listed on preregistration schedules and in catalogs will actually teach the courses. It can give cause to terminate a person's occupancy in a residence hall or even membership in the student body under extreme circumstances. It makes institutions meet standards of safety and security and students meet standards of social accountability. If we put it in writing, we take the mystery out of where we all stand. If we spell it out, we cover ourselves, If we keep our end of the bargain, we can walk through the valley of institutional evaluation by visiting committees and lawsuits and fear loss neither of academic standing nor of institutional assets nor of insurance coverage.

The problems with mere contractualism in colleges and universities are serious. The preoccupation with covering one's assets and maintaining prestige for the institution and of getting one's money's worth in grades and access to graduate schools and employment may blind us to the purpose of our joint endeavor and compromise the possibilities of community life. A covenantal understanding could take us beyond meeting minimal conditions to making maximal commitments.

A covenantal educational institution would be characterized by a profound gratitude for the traditions of learning, the generosity of benefactors, and the labors of parents and support staff, which enable the enterprise to exist. Students and teachers would appreciate what they owe each other and the students and teachers who have preceded them.

Covenant communities are not only conclaves of the grateful, they are unions of the faithful. Their common faith is not necessarily conformity to a single religious credo, although, in a broad sense, it has religious roots. It is commitment to the shared values that give the institution its roots and enable a community of learning to carry on its work with civility and integrity. To keep faith with the values that center the community is to keep faith with one another, and trust is based on the sense of our common commitment. In such a community, academic honesty, tolerance for different points of view, democratic participation, and concern for social justice are not just protections of individual interests dressed in fancy clothes; they are essential conditions for an institution where seeking truth is the mission.[33]

A covenanted institution will also go beyond minimalism by devoting itself to the total development of the person for the long haul, not just to the determination of a student's or professor's academic standing. Covenanters care about the reasons for absences and poor performance, about the burden imposed by holding a job while going to school, about what happens to a person who gets into trouble academically or socially, and about what happens to a graduate in searching for a job or moving to a new community.

President Truman reportedly said of one Latin American dictator, "He's an S.O.B., but he is our S.O.B." He was probably thinking contractually. "We need certain things from this guy so we shall hold our noses, avert our eyes, and keep the alliance alive a little longer." The dean of students who makes the same unflattering comment about a student may be thinking covenantally. Like members of a family, partners in covenant are, in a way, stuck with each other; they are committed to go the second mile to make things work out. Colleges that claim affiliation with covenantal religious traditions should be known by those fruits more than by the strictness of their rules and the orthodoxy of their faculties.

If the institution and the student join hands in mutual trust and care to seek each other's good, then mutual service will go beyond the minimum to the point of sacrifice. Students will be more likely to go all out to get everything they can from their courses and to give all they can to the enrichment of campus and community life. The institution will likewise make retention strategies and outcomes assessment more than simply means to demonstrate institutional quality to outside judges. These programs will also serve to monitor whether a school is doing all it can for those who have entrusted their college years and even their futures to it.

Contracts will continue to serve as hedges against our failures to be covenantal, but covenants will educate us beyond the limits of contracts. Not to continue to promote the covenantal model through community ritual, through staff selection and orientation, and through faculty interaction with students is to see our implicit and explicit contracts sink to something less than community. It is also to lose the normative pull of our noblest commitments against the practical drag of our preoccupations with achieving success and avoiding days in court.

Myth, Worldview, and Religion

Individualism is perhaps our most powerful cultural myth. We might better call it an ideology grounded and expressed in myth and story. Our "unalienable rights [to] life, liberty, and the pursuit of happiness," if set in a communitarian context, are the good news of this worldview. Respect for the dignity, autonomy, and privacy of each person and the fostering of everyone's creativity and individuality are values that we compromise only at our peril.[34] Our forebears came to these shores to claim them; they fought to assure them; they moved West to keep them. They are embodied in the Horatio Alger stories and in the American dream. They continue to attract the world's tired and poor. They continue to fuel the fires of ambition and creativity. Our individualism has effectively inoculated us against the collectivist or organic myths that reduce the individual to a tool of the state, a readily expendable martyr to the cause, or a cog in the machine.

There is also bad news, as the authors of *Habits of the Heart* elaborate. The dark side of individualism looms into view in the pursuit of one's own freedom at the expense of others, in the cruel devastation of Native Americans, in the exploitation of the environment, and in the ease with which we blame victims of poverty and injustice, as seen in Jules Feiffer's cartoon. The newest bane of individualism is what Michael Ignatieff calls the "medicalization" of it.[35] A swell of writing about health now manages to blame people for illness because they do not have a healthy frame of mind or the right personal habits. A good thing—that is, people taking more responsibility for their health—becomes a cruel thing, blaming the victim. If disease hits you, you not only have to shoulder the burden of the ailment; you also have to shoulder the blame for causing it, according to the self-mastery mentality.

When radical individualism reigns, the naked individual, stripped of all communal affiliations and institutional connections, becomes an abstraction, and society loses any reality save what contracting individuals give it. In large measure because of the countervailing images of the benevolent community and social justice provided by the biblical tradition, this radical individualism has often been balanced or corrected by a covenantal vision that is founded on gift rather than gain and opens community to all comers. We are a teamwork people as well as a get-ahead-of-your-neighbor people.

Contracts and covenants are not simply metaphors or models; they are expressions of basic myths or worldviews of a people. We are dealing, then, not merely with political culture, but also with people's fundamental orientations toward all of life, their worldviews, their religions. Whether we view people primarily as isolated individuals or as persons who find themselves in community with all its obligations and benefits is ultimately not just a political question; it is a religious or theological question. We may learn about living in covenant in the family or in a friendship or in some other social group and name no divine source or party to the covenant, but we are still dealing with basic worldviews, with matters of religious import, with whatever faith sets us in some ultimate context of meaning. James Fowler calls faith "a way *of knowing, of construing,* or *of interpreting* experience."[36] There is no unconstrued experience, and whatever myth we inhabit and whatever worldview we share provide a shared vision for a community. When we identify fully with a worldview, we have committed ourselves in a faith. How we see is who we are, and who we are is how we see.

What we make our center of loyalty determines what functions as religion for us, and that ultimate allegiance will determine which metaphors, models, or myths are considered authoritative when conflicts occur over who we should be and what we should do. Exposure to a variety of metaphors, models, and myths and to a variety of interpretations of the myth or worldview that gives us our bearings most basically can thwart us from deifying one metaphor, image, or model or one rendition of a worldview, but we still operate from some myth or outlook in any critique we attempt. Both covenantal traditions themselves and other traditions have cited the pitfalls of covenantal thinking. A covenantal outlook has, for instance, been used to justify the worst abuses of the "chosen people" mentality and to pit "us" against "them."

Metaphors, images, models, and myths can serve as mutual correctives without demanding the disappearance of the others. A rich religious tradition provides images, metaphors, and myths that are powerful enough to give guidance in our confusion and varied enough to keep the unfolding of truth a dynamic process. Only one basic myth or worldview, however, can ground one's integrity and frame one's outlook. As a guide to the moral life, the Bible's images, metaphors, and myths are probably more significant than its laws, principles, and rules. As Bruce Birch and Larry Rasmussen elaborate, the Bible promotes not just one dimension of our lives as moral agents, it promotes four: values, virtues, duties, and moral vision. Indirect moral formation from exposure to biblical psalms, stories, parables, and prophetic oracles in community worship is often more telling than direct moral exhortation.[37]

Since I have repeatedly pitted contracts and covenants against each other, it is worth saying that both models and both their underlying myths or worldviews (individualistic and communitarian) have important contributions to make. The beauty of contractualism is that it does establish rights or obligations that protect human dignity and well-being where they are in jeopardy. It lays down minimal conditions for interaction. It erects barriers against our tendencies to take advantage of each other. It stays oppression; it defines accountability; it sets limits to tolerance in situations where giving and taking have tended to become assigned roles rather than mutual reciprocations. Covenants need the contractual questions to keep covenants from taking the given for granted.

Contracts, nevertheless, need covenants to make them more than trade-offs. The contractual minimum usually falls short of a happy medium. From what the biblical traditions teach us about them, covenants belie the narcissism that has no historical memory and harbors no thought of future generations. They presuppose a social bond we did not create, while contracts presuppose a fundamental separation that individuals decide to forsake in their own best interests. Covenants remember a shared and gracious past that made a relationship possible. They locate grace within the limits of community life as well as in the heady exhilaration of liberation from bondage. They ask what is the most I can be in grateful response to what I have received, not just what is the least I must do to keep receiving my perks. Seeing life through covenantal eyes can give institutions a renewed sense of mission, professions a renewed sense of calling, and individualism a renewed sense of community.

Not only do our national morality tales and political myths reflect religious convictions or our substitutes for them, but our religious myths or worldviews also carry heavy ethical and political freight. For example, any religion or theology has to deal in some way with the problem of evil. Some religions regard evil as primarily the product of ignorance and believe that knowledge of the truth will bring peace to individuals and groups. When we fail to recognize the tenacity with which people cling to power ("rattlesnakes don't commit suicide") and the ingenuity with which we twist knowledge into shapes that serve our selfish ends, we doom ourselves to the disillusionment that seethes in the ruins of naïve utopianism. Belief that evil is really nonexistent once we come to see the truth will tend to issue in an apathetic acquiescence that may personally transcend suffering but will not change the conditions that caused it.

Accounting for evil by the presence of supernatural evil forces in the world will lead people to look for and label the satanic ones and justify any measures by the good people against those who are utterly evil. A vivid example is the Ayatollah Khomeini's order on February 14, 1989, that Muslims kill the author and the publishers of the novel *The Satanic Verses*, by Salman Rushdie. (If only he hadn't done it on Valentine's Day.) On the other hand, if evil in the world is an absurd and senseless presence from which we can expect no relief and for which there is no explanation (as in *The Plague*, by Albert Camus), then the appropriate response is heroic struggle against it with a smiling defiance that feels no sympathy from God.

If the chief cause of evil is dehumanizing social and political structures and the victims are not themselves corrupted by selfishness, pride, or sloth, then a true revolution could bring about an ideal social order. If evil is the result of universal human sinfulness that is evident both in individuals and their groups and institutions, then we shall want some hedges against people's impositions of their will on everyone else, and we shall know better than to divide the world neatly between members of the God Squad and those of the Evil Empire. As Reinhold Niebuhr posited, a biblical view of people as both created in God's image and fallen provides the foundation for democracy. Our capacity for justice makes self-government possible; but our inclination to injustice makes checks and balances necessary.[38] Our basic beliefs about the source, seriousness, and locus of evil profoundly influence our definition of moral problems and the ways we choose to address them.

The myths and worldviews the religious imagination provides also offer differing visions of the future—what is possible, likely, and desirable. If we can only expect everything to get worse until the inevitable, apocalyptic dropping of the curtain on history, we shall attend to our personal rectitude and even applaud the signs of the approaching end. If we trust in inevitable progress on the strength of further developments of technology and other exhibits of human ingenuity, we shall be tolerant of toxic wastes, environmental rapes, and other regrettable side effects in the fine print on the bottles containing the elixir of scientific salvation. If we envision the future in more cyclical and less linear terms, and feel the need to come to harmonious terms with the deaths and rebirths that characterize nature's ecology, we shall be less sanguine about doing everything we can do that tampers with nature. If we view the future as the unfolding of the consequences of human irresponsibility but also of human repentance (the view of the Hebrew prophets), we shall consider ourselves obligated to labor for justice and peace in the political arena since the future is open and prophets have offered visions of lions lying down with lambs and swords being beaten into plowshares and all people sitting unafraid under their own vines and fig trees. We not only act in response to a world our eyes enable us to see; we also act in anticipation of a world for which our vision enables us to hope. People do not hope for what they cannot imagine, and our images of a different future empower us to change things.

Measuring Our Imaginative Filters

As we have considered imaginative contexts of ethics as points of contact with the moral life and as points of view, we have both stated and implied that some metaphors, images, models, myths, and worldviews are better than others. If we do not believe it is sufficient to say "Everyone has her own slant on things, and who am I to judge?'' how can we elevate some imaginative filters over others? Saying that God told me so is a real discussion stopper, and some people in the Ku Klux Klan, among Afrikaner defenders of apartheid, and in Khomeini's entourage are all too certain that they act under divine orders. Saying that our scripture told us so is some protection against the strange private directives some people have heard, but the differences among scriptures, within scriptures, and in people's interpretations of scriptures do terminal damage to such claims in a pluralistic society. The basic convictions (rooted in myths and worldviews) that some call their religion and all of us practice as our equivalent of religion will be the arbiters among competing metaphors, models, and myths. Our imaginative filters of meaning reach for universal truth. They attempt to see and to say not just what is true for us but what is also true for all. And they may capture significant features of reality, but they do not capture it fully. There is no vantage point beyond all imaginative filters from which to make an objective evaluation of them, but some measures have emerged from our exploration, which for some of us are implications of the Christian story, but which are not the possession of only one mythic orientation or worldview.

Reich, for instance, shows that the stories we have been telling about ourselves as Americans have lagged behind what people are fond of calling "the real world." The global economic and political context has changed, but the American myths have not. Some people's ideas about poverty, welfare recipients, the effects of a nuclear exchange, women's "nature," and the Strategic Defense Initiative simply do not hold up under critical scrutiny. Granted that we all interpret studies and data through our own eyes, people of varying persuasions can at times agree that certain images and myths either lead us astray or do not have the validity they once did. "Bare facts" streak by so seldom that few catch sight of them, but our myths should help us make sense of what we experience and what careful studies discover and not blind us to what is going on. We see through our imaginative filters, but sometimes a contradiction overload raises enough questions to cause reassessment, if we are humble enough to acknowledge our limitations and if a promising alternative is available.

Humility is a cardinal virtue for the testing of our imaginative filters. If even a clock that is stopped is right twice a day, some other metaphors, images, models, and myths besides our favorites may have something to teach us, just as further critical study of human experience and the natural world may. Since we hold a worldview or use a model in the belief that it tells us truth, a tentative commitment would seem to be a contradiction in terms. Roger Shinn suggests that both faith and science can provide correctives for our ideologies, but he cautions both that ideology "determines the focus of scientific attention" and that "faith is already infused with ideology."[39] Still, faith is the companion of doubt, not its alternative. Criticism should not be excluded by commitment. Worldviews can invite internal criticism and external dialogue as well as discourage them.[40]

Integrity is another test of the character of our filters. We have noted several examples of images, models, and myths that falsely fragment people's lives. Maccoby's "gamesman" suffered from a head-heart split; radical individualism rends public and private life asunder; the biomedical model often isolates a disease from the person and the person's web of relationships. Whenever our imaginative filters fragment people into incompatible roles and their activities into irreconcilable or unconnected sectors, they deprive us of the ability to see life whole, and they contradict the covenantal concern we have advocated for the whole person and the whole of our existence.

The extent to which people are respected and vested with responsibility is another test of our imaginative filters. A seminary classmate of mine once penned a mock Calvinistic rendition of the hymn "Rise up, O Men of God." (It is true that the hymn was written for a men's convention, but why have we left it that way?) It read: "Sit down, O men of God; there is nothing you can do. We're all depraved, the elect are saved. What Calvin says is true." His was not an adequate summary of Calvin, but it is a telling slam at any worldview that makes human responsibility inconsequential and serves to denigrate and deactivate people rather than to empower and energize them. Whether it is nuclear war or the apocalypse that is inevitable, or whether it is an image of women or African-Americans or the poor that reduces them to passive acquiescence, any myth, image, or metaphor that consigns people to perennial childhood or turns the future into an unalterable fate is not only debilitating but also dehumanizing. People should be respected as persons of worth, potentiality, and accountability. People who have been victimized and deprived of their birthright as human beings should not be saddled with the blame for their plight, but neither should anyone belittle their ability to assume responsibility once the conditions of their oppression have been relieved through their efforts or those of others.

Honesty or realism about human potentiality for evil is another measure of the adequacy of our imaginative filters. The imagination should be playful in considering new options, but it serves us badly if it is naïve about the perversity of "good" people as well as "bad" people, about the arrogance of power and the lethargy of sloth, about the insidiousness of systemic evil and the stubbornness of entrenched interests. People are not only capable of assuming responsibility; they are also susceptible to demonstrating irresponsibility.

Looking at the world through rose-colored glasses is not the solution for the cynicism that looks at it through dark glasses.

Imagining people as related to others is another mark of an adequate outlook, of imaginative filters with "good character." As James Gustafson affirms, an interactional model makes more sense of human experience than either an individualistic, contractual model or an organic model. An individualistic model fails to see the self in its relatedness, and the organic model reduces the self to its function in the larger whole.[41] In the terminology of *Habits of the Heart*, this measure tells us why biblical and civic individualism have it over utilitarian and expressive individualism. People find themselves in community, in relatedness to others and the world around them, not in removed insularity.

Faith is also a measure of the character of our imaginative filters, our metaphoric and mythic outlooks. As we have said, our worldviews express some faith, some way of construing the world. The question is, What is the center of loyalty and value presupposed by this outlook or worldview? Does the ideology or myth or worldview demand or expect that we give ultimate allegiance to some finite human good? If nation or creed or economic system or race or political affiliation or institutional success or personal power is accorded the place of God in a worldview or myth or ideology, then that center of value deserves repudiation for its eccentricity. Its focus is off center. But of course concentration on a different center would make a person resistant to admitting its feet of clay.

Reach or inclusiveness is another critical measure of myth. The virtue in question is love or intensive and extensive care. Our myths should prompt us to care deeply and to care broadly. They should expand the scope of our responsibility and concern for others. If our myths enable us to overlook the stories and feelings of some people, they are flawed. Hendrik Hertzberg observes that "many of our reigning national myths, important parts of America's civil religion, simply exclude black people." Calling ourselves a "nation of immigrants" and the "land of opportunity" overlooks the fact that we are also a nation of slaves and that some of our forebears came here in chains, not in search of opportunity. We will not find the political will to heal the wound of race "until whites and blacks can agree that they are citizens of the same country." We need "a refurbished national mythology that takes in the historical experience of all Americans."[42] If our general outlook justifies exclusion of certain groups, nations, races, religions, or individuals from the circle of community and the reach of compassion, it forfeits its claim on us. If it reinforces our proclivity for pitting "us" against "them," whether "they" are "the Rot at the Top," "the Mob at the Gates," the drones in the economy, "the other America," or some other "other," it leads us astray. When we use images (such as "the global village" or "spaceship earth") or tell stories of mutual trust and mutual obligation about America, we build human solidarity instead of perpetuating polarization and giving it religious justification.

Joseph Campbell observes that in most myths brotherhood is "confined to a bounded community." Beirut epitomizes the clash of closed circles—Christianity, Islam, and Judaism—each saying, "We are the chosen group, and we have God."[43] Only a mythology of the planet will do for the future, and Campbell did not, at the time of his death in 1987, believe we have such a mythology available at present. Buddhism comes closest because it recognizes all beings as Buddha beings. The earth seen from space might, he believed, be the symbol of the new mythology to come.[44] I want to believe that he sold short the inclusive possibilities in Christianity, Islam, and Judaism, but he had plenty of historical evidence to support him.

Hope is our final measure. What futures do our myths and worldviews and ideologies imagine and enable? Are future generations taken into account? Is the sustainability of life on the planet accorded grave importance? Is the future open to meaningful steps toward human liberation and world peace, or do we simply await "the big whoosh"? A myth or a worldview should be known not only by the company it keeps but also by the horizon it sees.

If you say that I am only trotting out moral measures of myth from the mythic milieu I inhabit as part of the Christian tradition and as part of the American civil religion and as part of the Western liberal democratic ideology and so forth, you are right. I am situated in making my assessment as we all are. Nevertheless, I am also selective—not by assuming a lofty perch beyond all myths, worldviews, and ideologies, but by letting different traditions or stories act as correctives to one another. Our membership in several communities of moral meaning sets us in plural myths and ideologies. Our exposure to other communities in our shrinking world gives us additional perspective on ourselves. Christianity, American civil religion, and Western democratic political theory have been mixed blessings to our race and our planet, and I have tried to let criticisms from other quarters shape my appropriation of those traditions. Only to the extent that we hear other voices and see from other vantage points can we see around the blinders that our locations impose. In the next chapter we shall consider not only what it means to be stopped in our own tracks but what it might mean to stand in others' shoes.

Summary

Our myths, worldviews, and ideologies are the foundations of our moralities. The seeing they allow and enable precedes further action. Differences in faith and moral vision are more critical than differences over specific ethical questions. And the differences in faith are not only divisions over the gods we trust; they are also conflicts over the way we put our trust in the same God. The task of doing ethics cannot be left solely to the imagination. There are issues to sort out and situations to interpret and hard choices to make, but until we take into account the myths, worldviews, models, images, and metaphors that enable and shape moral perception, we are taking ethics out of context.

6
Life Stories as Contexts: Transmigration of Stories

"And it shook me. A tiny brick house with two rooms. No ceiling, no electricity, concrete floor. In the dining room there was a table covered with a piece of linoleum and two rickety chairs, I think, and a small cupboard of crockery; and in the other room a single bed and some paraffin boxes. That was all. That was where she lived, with her husband and their three youngest children and two of her husband's sisters. They took turns with the bed; the rest slept on the floor. There were no mattresses. It was winter, and the children were coughing." Her voice suddenly choked. "Do you understand? It wasn't the poverty as such: one knows about poverty, one reads the newspaper, one isn't blind, one even has a 'social conscience.' But Dorothy [her family's housemaid for years] was someone I thought I *knew*; she'd helped Dad to bring me up; she lived with me in the same house every day of my life. You know, it felt like the first time I'd ever really looked right into someone else's life. As if, for the first time, I made the discovery that other lives *existed*. And worst of all was the feeling that I knew just as little about my own life as about theirs."

Melanie Brewer, a journalist,
in Andre Brink's A Dry White Season

We not only inhabit institutional worlds and imaginative worlds of metaphor and myth; we inhabit the histories we are making as persons and groups. What we are living through is our point of contact for the moral life; what we have lived through gives us a point of view on the moral questions we face. Experience may not always teach us best, but it teaches us most. Learning how many people in prison were abused as children and how many of them have learning disabilities tells us how much we are the product of what has happened to us. We help write our own scripts, and we act as we "see fit" in those scripts, but much of our story has been written for us by accidents of birth. We experience the world as male or female, as siblings or as only children, as mothered and fathered or as lacking one or both parents, as rich or poor or in-between, as well nourished or as malnourished, as healthy or unhealthy, as educated or uneducated or poorly educated, as part of a race, as part of a nation, as part of a religious community or not a part, as trusted and trusting or as betrayed and suspicious, and as loved or hated or ignored.

Within those general categories, we have lived our unique combinations of experiences. We have had not just diseases, but our particular illnesses. Taking a case history virtually means taking a life history if you believe that illness is "a drama in the narrative of a life."[1] Studying cases in ethics is likewise superficial if it does not encompass the studying of lives. To look at actual people's lives is to consider not failures and successes in general, but particular ones; not grief in general, but particular losses; not friendship in general, but unique clusters of close relationships; not a type of education, but an education at a particular college and a particular professional school.

An old friend of mine once told me that he had always felt like more an outsider than an insider because he changed schools every two weeks during the early years of his education. His family ran a "Wild West" show, and they saw to it that he was in school, but he quit learning the teachers' names because he knew he would soon be gone.

Another friend of mine has never forgotten the night during World War II when a Japanese-American girl from an internment camp was visiting in his town as a guest of his church, and he took her to a movie at the request of the director of Christian education for the congregation. As he walked down the street with her and felt the stares of his fellow teenagers in his South Carolina town, he saw racism from a new perspective.

For most young people of draft age during the Vietnam War, their decision about participation was not about pacifism and war in general but about that particular war and their participation in it. For a pregnant thirteen year old, abortion is no abstract moral question, it is a personal trauma. What we see as our duties, our aims, our identity, and our role models is mediated by our own life story. Where we have been and where we think we are going shape our options and our decisions about the next step.

In the mid-1970s an ugly confrontation erupted between the United Mine Workers and the Duke Power Company in Harlan County, Kentucky. One hundred and sixty miners went on strike against Eastover Mining Company, a Duke Power subsidiary, over whether the company would sign a union contract that the UMW supported 113 to 55. There, in traditionally union-busting and bloody Harlan County, the workers had previously been represented by a company-oriented local known as the Southern Labor Union, but they had become unhappy with the hospitalization and medical benefits of SLU, with the failure of SLU to demand portal-to-portal pay from the company, and with SLU's refusal to take Eastover to task for repeated safety violations (ten citations for major violations by the U.S. Mine Enforcement Safety Administration between October 1972 and June 1973, when the election took place).

One of the central figures in the negotiations was Norman Yarborough, founder and president of Eastover, who represented Duke Power. The miners found him difficult and intransigent. He argued "law and order," calling the illegal picketing and the use of switches by some women on substitute workers (called "scabs" by the strikers) a "dire threat to our American way of life." He termed the picketing "illegal" because the number of participants exceeded prescribed limits if the crowd that congregated near designated picket points was included in the count. The reason Yarborough is significant for our discussion is not that he took such a dim view of the picketers and the UMW supporters, but that he had a personal story that shaped his perceptions. He felt that he had done much for "his" workers and their families, and that they were ungrateful. He also remembered with bitterness his father's experience with the UMW. A dyed-in-the-wool member of the union, his father had even been an organizer at one time. Yet when he became disabled, the UMW would not pay his hospital bill. Behind Yarborough's stance lay that story.

Mary Widner, one of the women arrested for assault and battery (with a switch), had a different story. Her husband, Ray, a long-time member and committeeman with the AFL-CIO before coming to work at Brookside Mine, had been idled by a bullet wound in an accident not directly related to the strike. He was also under injunction to desist from strike activities because he was charged with assaulting a strikebreaker. He and Mary lived near company headquarters, and he carried a revolver when he was in his house. He was proud of his wife's arrest. She said the women used switches because "they [the strikebreakers] started something." Ray stated, "One got smart with my wife, and she whipped him. They tried to talk to them right, but they wouldn't listen, and the women switched 'em. Next morning they used switches on 'em again. Since these women took over, ain't nobody been working."

Yarborough admitted that the guards his company hired were not "Sunday school teachers," but he was convinced that they were needed for "a mob of people that's got no respect for the law." The strikers called the guards "gun thugs," and shooting incidents included at least one firing on a miner's car.

Mrs. Widner, who had been arrested for violating the injunction and ordered not to engage in strike activities, and other women continued to make coffee each morning for the fifty to sixty women and other strike supporters who gathered around the mine entrance to "persuade" scabs not to work. The pastor of a local Baptist church, himself a UMW member for thirty years, held "sunrise worship services" near the mine entrances. A mob from one person's perspective was a worshiping community from another's perspective.[2] The differences in perspective are not unusual. After all, one group of Americans regards Oliver North as a hero and a patriot and another views him as a liar and a subverter of the intentions of the U.S. Congress. The notable ingredient in the story is the importance of personal experience in the shaping of attitudes and actions. To understand ourselves and others and our conflicts with each other over our interpretations of moral problems and our responses to them, we must delve into people's remembered pasts and foreseen futures, including our own.

Standing in Others' Shoes

The differences between Yarborough and the Widners would not necessarily have gone away if they had come to a better understanding of the level of intensity in the feelings on each side of the conflict. During the critical confrontations in the late 1950s and early 1960s between the Student Nonviolent Coordinating Committee and the Southern Christian Leadership Conference on one side and such law enforcement officers as "Bull" Conner and Jim Clark and such governors as James Patterson and Ross Barnett on the other side, if John Lewis and Martin Luther King, Jr., had sat down with their antagonists to listen to each other's stories, we have no guarantee that they would have come to see eye to eye and that civil rights for all Americans would have been accepted without violence and upheaval. Nevertheless, as long as we remain imprisoned in our own prejudices and encased in our own stories, we are doomed to persist in the injustices they justify.

Either coercion or withdrawal, the extreme opposing responses to conflict, may be the appropriate choices in a situation, but, as the authors of *Women's Ways of Knowing* affirm, "Dialogue is the primary means of preventing and resolving conflict," and dialogue entails the sharing of stories as well as the pitting of positions against each other.[3] In contrast to riots, the nonviolent civil rights demonstrations were efforts to dramatize a story and to tell it in the language of the Bible and of the Constitution and the Bill of Rights, which were part of the stories of the oppressors. Another story, the demonstrators found out, was closer to the hearts of their adversaries. Their traditional way of life blinded and deafened the arch-opponents to the message of the demonstrations. If, as Thomas Ogletree states, "to be moral is to be hospitable to the stranger,"[4] being moral requires not only our respect for the person of the other but also our openness to the world of the other.

In my days of doctoral study, I was sometimes asked to lead "junior church" in the congregation where I worked on weekends. During the sermon in the sanctuary, my crew and I would retire to my office on those Sundays for some education and diversion until the service ended. One snowy day, I had worn some rubber boots over my shoes, and I stashed them behind the door in my office. My plan on this particular occasion was to engage the little group in a discussion of what love is. The discussion did not get off to a very auspicious start, and soon any hopes I entertained of new breakthroughs in understanding were getting dashed by the activities of one little guy. He was searching my desk drawers, climbing the bookshelves, and successfully diverting the group's attention as I repeatedly sought to get him involved. His master stroke of disruption was putting on my boots and clomping around the room. With an unusual flash of inspiration, I countered with a master move of my own. I made him the hero by announcing that he had given the best answer of all, because "Love is putting yourself in someone else's shoes." For a moment, at least, we were a group again, and he had our attention for good reason.

Trying to occupy the shoes or look through the eyes of the other may be only a strategy for outwitting an enemy or discovering more fiendish ways to torment someone we hate, but entering the other's world is usually both an evidence of care and a stimulus to care. Love attempts to stand in the other's shoes in order to treat the person as that person would want to be treated, and finding out what it is like in another's shoes can move us to loving action.

In her January 19, 1990, presidential address to the Society of Christian Ethics, "Love Your Enemy: Sex, Power, and Christian Ethics," Karen Lebacqz took telling exception to the blanket admonition to assume the viewpoint of the other. Citing the example of the sexually assaulted wife who is intimidated into losing her own perspective because "he (her husband) says it didn't happen that way," she argued that the self is endangered when people are abstracted from the concrete historical realities that have shaped them. Loving "the enemy" who has violated you should not require abandonment of your own perspective. It is crucial for such women and all whose personhood is threatened to "hold on to their own considered rights and interests." Lebacqz fears that the relational ethics of caring as

advocated by Nel Noddings and others may neglect the need to hold
one's ground against "the enemy," to stand behind one's own perspective.

Putting ourselves in the other person's shoes should not require
the repudiation of our own standpoint and wholesale adoption of the
other's. Nevertheless, true dialogue does require "being moved" in
order to hear "where the other is coming from." When people enjoy positions of power and privilege, it is particularly crucial to
fathom the experience of the powerless, the vulnerable, and the
deprived. Lebacqz rightly cautions against the self-effacement of
adopting the perspective of those who come down or look down on
us, but there is still a moral mandate to learn the other's view. One
admonition insists that we keep loving ourselves, the other that we
reach out to the neighbor and even the enemy. Love can have it
both ways.

In his book *Black Robes, White Justice*, Bruce Wright, one of the
few black jurists in our nation, questions a system in which male,
white, middle-class, conservative judges pass judgment on a parade
of dark-skinned defendants whose way of life is like a foreign country to the jurists. Similarly, white law-enforcement officers do not
fathom the violence of racism as they deal with minority offenders
against "law and order."[5] In the movie *Cry Freedom*, Stephen Biko,
who died of beatings he received in a South African prison because
of his opposition to apartheid, states to a white audience, "We know
how you live. Ninety percent of you have no idea how we live." In
the movie, and in real life, white journalist Donald Woods does discover how blacks live and die in his country, and he is moved to
action as a result. He not only takes a stand through his paper, he
also writes and smuggles out his exposé concerning Biko's death, at
great risk to himself and his family.

Andre Brink's *A Dry White Season*, which is quoted at the head of
the chapter, is a fictional account of a similar awakening. In the
novel, the main character, Ben du Toit, is an ordinary, decent, harm-
less Afrikaner who teaches school and considers a black janitor, Gordon Ngubene, his friend. First, Gordon's son Jonathan, whose
education Ben had financed, dies in police custody. When Gordon
dies under the same circumstances after he probes too deeply in his
investigation of his son's death, Ben becomes a relentless searcher
for the truth about both deaths. His initial faith in the basic justice of
the governmental system is destroyed, and he becomes alienated
from his family, his principal, his teaching colleagues, and his
church, as well as his government. He resolves to uncover the causes
of the deaths and to exonerate the victims of the implication that
they were communist agents, communist dupes, or suicides, and he
eventually loses his own life as a result.

As Ben begins his search, he makes his first visit to the black township of Soweto, where Gordon and his family lived.

> He felt like a visitor from a distant land arriving in a city where all the inhabitants had been overcome by the plague. All the symptoms of life had been preserved intact, but no living creature had survived the disaster. He was alone in an incomprehensible expanse. And it was only much later, when he returned to his study—and even that appeared foreign, not his own, but belonging to a stranger, a room where he was not the master but the intruder—that his thoughts began to flow again.[6]

He had known Gordon, he thought, but he had not really known the man's private existence. He discovers "not just another city, but another country, another dimension, a wholly different world." He feels that he has landed on "the dark side of the moon." What he considered unbelievable or at least unusual happens all the time there. When he returns home he feels as if he has never seen it before. He looks into the mirror and sees a total stranger.[7] His life has been turned around as radically as that of Melanie Brewer, his ally, whose experience is described in the opening quotation.

Being Born Again

Ben had transmigrated to the world of his black friends and could never see his own world in the same way as before. There are people who believe that souls can move from one body to another, and some movie scripts have experimented with that possibility with forgettable, though somewhat humorous, results. What we are broaching here is a transmigration with much greater promise and none of the abuses of those who claim that people from other eras are living in them now. We are talking about the transmigration of selves to other stories. John Dunne might speak of these experiences as "passing over," the language he uses to describe migration into the world and worldview of another religion. We pass over as the Christians or Christian atheists or Buddhists we are to explore another worldview. We are free to return to our own religious traditions after such a trip, but we are never the same again, if we have truly exposed ourselves to the world of the other.[8] If we decide to stay in the world to which we passed, it is also true that we will never be the same as those who have always been there. We shall always carry the imprint of our origins.

We might also call such experiences as Brink captures "being born again." Ben and Melanie not only discovered the other, they found themselves. They could never be the same again; their old haunts looked strange to them. In his exposition of the Fourth Gospel in *Liberation Theology: Liberation in Light of the Fourth Gospel,* Frederick Herzog describes the new birth described in the third chapter of John as a new corporateness. For him, to be reborn is to become black, or Native American, or Vietnamese peasant, or Soviet Jew and thereby to find a new selfhood.[9] A new solidarity with oppressed people is a new birth.

In *The Power of Myth*, Joseph Campbell observes that the Buddhist, Greek, and Christian mythologies all include virgin births. He finds a common meaning in this birth that means dying to one's animal nature and coming to live as "a human incarnation of compassion." The god who is born, he claims, is each of us in a second birth. Our humanity truly begins when we live not for self-preservation, not for sex and procreation, and not to master others, but *for* others. To live from the heart is to share the suffering of others. Compassion is "experienced participation in the suffering of another person."[10] Arguing about his blended interpretation of these myths would divert us from our central concern. The point is that whether we are called to become Christ or Buddha or simply a neighbor to our neighbors, participation in the suffering of others is the essence of spiritual life.

In the mid-1950s a symbiotic relationship developed between national television coverage and the civil rights movement, and the changed position of the camera had a dramatic effect on the conscience of the nation. Henry Hampton explains:

> In the beginning of the movement, in stories about the Supreme Court's Brown decision, which outlawed segregation in public schools, and in stories surrounding the lynching of 14-year-old Emmett Till, the cameras record basically a white point of view, showing the black characters sympathetically and white racists as they were. As the civil-rights movement heats up and it grows increasingly clear where the violence lies, the cameras move behind the march leaders and look outward at the hostile sheriffs and their deputies.
>
> Later, when "black power" becomes the cry of persistent activists, it is easy to log the shift of the cameras away from the movement point of view and back toward the middle. By the time of the 1967 riots (for the record, many blacks still choose to call them rebellions), the camera's point of view is from behind the police lines aimed outward at the rioters. For white Americans, it is a return to the old racial nightmare, the point of view of George Armstrong Custer.[11]

Hampton, who was executive producer of "Eyes on the Prize," the 1987 documentary series, calls the camera lens a "two-edged sword" because its positioning "can either distance blacks and whites, or help introduce them to each other's reality." And the subtle message of the camera's point of view is "whose world this is and who controls it."[12]

Why does liberation theology push a "preferential option for the

poor," as the U.S. Catholic Bishops have worded it in their statement on economic justice?[13] Why is solidarity with those oppressed
economically, politically, racially, or sexually more of a new birth
than getting to know a new roommate in college, or falling in love,
or studying a new discipline, or learning a new language, or living in
a different religious community, or having a coronary bypass operation? All of these are eye-opening and life-changing experiences.

One reason is that experiencing even a sample of the hurt, deprivation, and dehumanization of others jars us by its ugliness and by
the possibility that our relative privilege and power have contributed to the problem more than to the solutions. Where people lack
the minimal conditions for subsistence, health, shelter, political
freedom, and economic opportunity, their plight has the strongest
claim on our attention; that is, unless we can comfort ourselves with
the explanation that those people brought it all on themselves. What
is more, there are more of "them" than there are of "us" (if you
happen to be a North American white person living in relative afflu-
ence, as the writer of these lines is). If we have no idea how the
other much-more-than-half lives, we are not in touch with the real
world.

Still another reason is that the lenses that those on the bottom
offer us give us twice as much for our money. G. F. Hegel, W. E. B.
DuBois, and Karl Marx point out that the slave or other oppressed
person knows two worlds: the master's world, which the slave must
know to survive, and the world of oppression, which the oppressed
cannot help knowing.[14] The new birth through solidarity puts our
"taken-for-granted" world under critical scrutiny while it also
reveals a previously unknown experience to us.

Being born again ethically is not just an errand of mercy for the
powerful and the privileged, it is a journey of self-discovery. Work
among the homeless and the hungry, try to survive for a month on
Aid to Families with Dependent Children and food stamps, experience fear as a racial minority in a strange and hostile place, get
seriously ill when you are unemployed and no longer covered by
health insurance, spend time with AIDS sufferers, and you come to
view differently not only others but also yourself.

What of our various roles of power and privilege? Does not the
doctor need to see through the patient's eyes, the lawyer through
the client's eyes, the teacher through the student's eyes, the bureaucrat through the eyes of the person who is supposedly being served
by the bureaucracy, the owner or manager through the eyes of the
employee, the male through the eyes of the female, the parent
through the eyes of the child? *Heartsounds* is a moving account by
his wife of a surgeon's own experience with heart disease.[15] Finding
out what people endured as well as received from his medical col-

leagues and the hospital staffs with whom they work was shocking to him and his wife. Had he been able to return to the practice of his profession, he would not have been the same doctor. A 1989 citation of the toughest bosses in America included one North Carolina executive who was referred to as "Commando" by his subordinates. He had something to learn from listening to them.

Getting Into Others' Shoes

Michael Ignatieff speaks of the "limited ability of humans to put themselves in each other's skin."[16] He is talking about the problem of entering the "foreign country" of the cancer patient, for example, if we have not suffered the same illness. However, any effort to get into the shoes or skins of others is fraught with huge difficulties, and some would call it an exercise in futility. After all, the privileged person who spends time in a ghetto can always leave, the teacher who tries to identify with students does not have to take the final exam and get a grade on a transcript that might have significant bearing on future schooling or employment, and the doctor who listens sensitively to patients is still the doctor. Furthermore, the white person is still white, the American is still an American, and the Christian explorer of Buddhism is still the *Christian* explorer no matter how deep one's sympathies run. Ian Barbour puts the matter well: "He can never completely enter the interpretive framework of a culture vastly different from his own. But he can so immerse himself in its life and thought that he can sympathetically imagine how the world would look from another's perspective."[17]

Developmental psychologists would say that it takes going through several stages to arrive in those other shoes if we ever make it at all, and few would claim that it comes naturally. Particularly if we are talking about the shoes and skins of people very different from ourselves, some "affirmative action" is necessary if we are to escape the captivity of our own stories and broaden our experience. Affirmative action, in this case, means going out of our way to learn how the homeless, the hungry, the least advantaged, and other cultures live. It can include intentional exposure of ourselves and others, such as the people we teach in our institutions or the people who work in them, to lives foreign to our experience. What kinds of field trips and internships and research projects do we include in the education and orientation of people whose job it is or will be to serve populations to which they have had negligible exposure on any terms but their own? Different behaving could bring different seeing.

Even without leaving home or school, we can take affirmative action. The right films and videotapes have changed peoples' perspectives permanently. The son of a friend resolved to go to Africa after seeing *Cry, Freedom*. Viewing the "Eyes on the Prize" series has changed people's perceptions and reoriented their lives. Visual exposure to mass starvation and malnutrition in Bangladesh or Sudan has reoriented people. It is also true that we have practiced skills at turning off and tuning out what we would rather not see and hear. Although shocking encounters have triggered radical rebirths, the willingness and capacity to put ourselves in others' shoes are in some ways acquired abilities and disciplines.

Daniel Coleman, writing in *The New York Times*, has surveyed recent scientific studies that have taken clear exception to the conventional wisdom about the roots of empathy—the ability to feel what another is feeling. Psychiatrist Leslie Brothers of the California Institute of Technology has found that monkeys will prevent other monkeys from receiving electrical shocks in response to the distress on another's face. Research on the human brain suggests that certain areas, the visual cortex and the amygdala, register and respond to others' emotions. Edmund Rolls, a neuroscientist at Oxford University, has discovered that certain neurons respond to others' grimaces. Although infants and toddlers have long been considered incapable of empathy and the age of seven or eight was pegged as the time when cognitive development made such feeling possible, psychologist Martin Hoffman has observed newborns crying more loudly when other babies cried than when a computer simulated infants' cries or another equally loud noise disturbed them. A nine-month-old has crawled to her mother for comfort at the sight of another child's fall. Hoffman saw a one-year-old bring his mother to comfort a fellow infant even though the sufferer's own mother was in the room. A fifteen-month-old has brought a teddy bear and a security blanket to a hurt friend. Although infants are at first confused about whose pain the hurt is, two-and-a-half-year-olds understand that another's pain is the problem. These children manifest differing degrees of awareness of others' plights depending both on the way they are raised and on differences in their brains, and of course adults exhibit great variations in moral awareness. As Coleman explains, criminal sociopaths show no concern for victims, and both the chemically schizophrenic and the autistic show empathy deficits. Empathy may even become a means of exploiting and manipulating others rather than a way of compassion.[18]

Such findings lend support to the claims of Adam Smith in the eighteenth century (*The Theory of Moral Sentiments*) and Larry Churchill in our own time (*Rationing Health Care in America*) that sympathy (which we here treat as synonymous with empathy) is a natural capacity of our social nature rather than a virtue. According to Churchill, "the imaginative capacity to put ourselves in each other's shoes" is what makes the virtues of justice and benevolence possible. These virtues extend our concern for others beyond the range of our direct experiences of others' anguish. They emerge with our ability to scrutinize our actions from our society's perspective and to encompass people in our concern who are outside our realm of direct exposure, but they are rooted in our social relatedness, not in our ability to detach ourselves from all connections and think "objectively."[19] Our early empathy does not automatically develop into compassion, but it testifies that social solidarity is not something we decide to create, but something we learn to extend.

Developmental psychologist Robert Selman chooses not to concentrate on empathy for the feelings of others, but instead to trace stages in the ability to take other perspectives than one's own.[20] He believes that elementary school children can be assisted to higher levels of perspective-taking if educators know what they are doing. Between ages four and six, children are egocentric in their perspective-taking. They know there are other perspectives, but they assume that the others are identical to theirs (Level 0). Between ages six and eight, "subjective perspective-taking" develops (Level 1). Now the child recognizes that other people are in different situations and have different information and that they therefore may see things differently. At Level 2 (roughly ages eight to ten) the child can do "self-reflective perspective-taking." Now children can reflect on their own feelings and thoughts and act in anticipation of others' responses to them.

Level 3 (ages ten to twelve) he calls "mutual perspective-taking." The child takes a third person's point of view and realizes that two persons can put themselves in each other's places before deciding how to react. At Level 4 ("qualitative-system perspective-taking"), the adolescent discerns not only mutual expectations between people but deeper levels and even multiple systems of perspective-taking. People discern levels within themselves and others that are more complicated than consideration of others' actions from their perspective before reacting. A complex network or system connects our interactions. We take account of others' perspective-taking and recognize that we always have a perspective in our own taking of others' perspectives. At Level 5 ("symbolic interaction perspective-taking"), perspective-taking is a method for analyzing social relations. The use of similar processes of analysis supposedly leads to mutual understanding.

Selman finds that a particular child rarely operates only at one level, that children develop at different rates, and that a child may be functioning at different levels depending on what the child is reasoning about. Above all, he emphasizes that experience plays a critical role in this development. It is not a simple biological process.

As other developmental theorists have concluded, Selman posits that development is apt to occur when conflict puts a person in an intellectual or social dilemma and the person is exposed to another level of perspective-taking. The method that was employed in his experiments involved showing a filmstrip that presents an open-ended social or moral dilemma. Guided peer-group discussion then gave the kids the chance to try out their views and hear those of others. Role playing also assisted perspective-taking.

One-shot efforts did not effect significant change, and significant development became apparent only six to eight months after the strategy had been introduced into the fabric of daily classroom activity. Achieving higher levels of perspective-taking did not guarantee that moral thought had progressed to an equivalent degree. Some delinquents showed perspective-taking equal to their peers, yet they did not draw the connection between perspective-taking and moral judgment.[21] Still, elementary training in perspective-taking is the basis for later moral education in junior and senior high school. There are no guarantees that any educational program will make moral sensitivity develop, yet Selman's work suggests that we need to reckon with some developmental needs that must be met before moral maturation can occur.

Women's Ways of Knowing offers educational insights for later stages in the educational process. The best knowing puts listening and speaking in balance. Empowering people who have been reduced to silence or kept in it by others' attitudes toward them requires active, empathetic listening to people on their terms. Moved by "attentive caring" (for the written word, ideas, and objects as well as for people), the true listener practices "forbearance." Refusing to judge and abstaining from exercising control, the empowering teacher will enable people to find their voices by seeing and hearing them on their terms.

The student has something to learn from others, including the teacher, but until a person is valued as a speaker, there is no genuine partner for a dialogue. To hear more than information, we need first to be heard. As we established earlier, the authors advocate connected knowing over separate knowing. Connected knowers imagine themselves into an author's mind and believe that seeing the personality behind the position or poem adds to the perception. Separate knowers try to subtract the personality of the perceiver because they want to purify perception of any slant. Both kinds of knowers get out from behind their own eyes and use a different vantage point. The separated knowers use the lens of a discipline (how sociology sees the problem), but connected knowers attempt to see through the eyes of the other person, a threatening prospect to many persons who view learning as a less intimate enterprise.[22]

Empathetic listening is as crucial for a doctor's relationship to a patient and to a patient's family as it is for a teacher's relationship to a student. In his discussion of the clinical encounter between doctors and patients, families, and colleagues, Richard Zaner insists that doctors both can and should put themselves in the shoes of those they seek to help. Doctors cannot experience every condition their patients do, but their common human experience provides a point of contact. If the professional caregivers will attend carefully to what the patients and family members are saying and otherwise communicating (by gesture, posture, facial expression, and silence), they will be able to help with illnesses and not just treat diseases. "Affiliative feeling" means continuing to ask the patients to tell not only what their symptoms are but how they feel about them. With physician Eric Cassell, Zaner insists not only that the other's world is accessible to us but that a disciplined effort to understand it is morally obligatory. The act of putting oneself in another's shoes is "a, if not *the*, fundamental moral act."[23]

The move to the other's shoes through empathetic listening is not, then, the peculiar obligation of teachers and doctors. In any professional relationship there is often a perceived imbalance of power and knowledge that reduces the layperson to silence. Just as a good parent wants above all to see a daughter or son become a mature adult, caring professionals will strive to empower those who entrust them with their needs and problems. Further, the whole of the moral life should be characterized by attentive listening and seeing. As Nel Noddings tells us, empathy "does not involve projection but reception." "I do not project, I receive the other into myself, and I see and feel with the other."[24]

The attitude she describes recalls the *aggiornamento* of Pope John XXIII as he guided the Second Vatican Council to open the windows and let the outside winds blow into the church he headed. Other Christians became "separated brethren" instead of heretics. It also recalls Kurt Vonnegut's science fiction–writing source of wisdom, Kilgore Trout, who said, "All of these years, I have been opening the window and making love to the world."[25]

Of course, in order for us to entertain others' outlooks as claims on our attention, we have to entertain the possibility that our versions of the truth are at best incomplete, at least biased, and at worst warped. In the Christian story, such an admission is made possible by the assurance that people are accepted, forgiven, and affirmed in spite of themselves. Knowing that their worth is not dependent on their goodness or rightness enables people to admit the possibility that they have been in the wrong both in their outlooks and their actions. Justification by grace through faith takes a person off the defensive. People who have all the answers and see others as having nothing to give them that they need will not be good listeners anywhere. If we are defensive whenever anyone takes exception to "the conventional wisdom," we will be loath to receive new light from any source, especially from those that are strangest to us.

In his exposition of "hospitality to the stranger," Thomas Ogletree makes effective use of "the hermeneutics of suspicion" (a contribution from Paul Ricoeur).[26] This suspicion refuses to concede finality to the conventional wisdom. A healthy dose of humility about our slant on things and of skepticism about the conventional wisdom that our comfortable circles of association reinforce may not be the beginning of wisdom, but it is a basic prerequisite. As Philip Keane suggests, a playful imagination that suspends judgment is an excellent preventive against getting stuck in the conventional wisdom.[27] We can play different dimensions of our experience off against each other. We can experiment with different metaphors and listen to new stories with a certain abandon that need not forsake the values of the traditional or the wisdom that resides in many conventions. The nonchalance of faith makes this playfulness possible. Inhospitality to the other (even the otherness in ourselves) robs us of a broader perspective on the world at the same time that it robs other lives of our expressions of care.

The depth of the loss we incur by our inhospitality to the stranger is dramatically presented in John Updike's short story "The Christian Roommates," which is set in the early 1960s.[28] Orson Ziegler arrives at Harvard, with a "vaguely irritated squint," from a small South Dakota town. There his father was the doctor, his family was Methodist, and he had been class president, valedictorian, and captain of the football and baseball teams. It had bothered him that the basketball captain, the only boy he had known who was better than he was at anything important, was Lester Spotted Elk, "a full-blooded Chippewa with dirty fingernails and brilliant teeth, a smoker, a drinker, a discipline problem." It would turn out that someone far more bothersome was waiting to be his roommate.

Entering his room, he finds Henry "Hub" Palamountain, the self-converted Episcopalian from Oregon with whom he had been paired (presumably because both were Protestant Christians from west of the Mississippi). His roommate, sitting barefoot before a spinning wheel, leaps to his feet to reveal a getup that included pegged sky-blue slacks, a lumberjack shirt with a silk foulard at the neck, and a white Nehru cap. Before shaking hands, Hub puts his palms together, bows, and murmurs something inaudible to Orson. The thick lenses of his glasses accentuate "the hyperthyroid bulge of his eyes and their fishy, searching expression." Hub, it turns out, is "an Anglican Christian Platonist strongly influenced by Gandhi." He has hitchhiked across the country to Harvard, requesting that his plane

fare be given to the Indian Relief Fund. He does yoga. He is a vege-
tarian. He prays kneeling beside his bed and lying across it with his
arms spread. He has spent two years working as a gluer in a plywood
mill. He has memorized nearly all of the *Phaedo* in Greek while
working inside a gluer machine and possesses several volumes of
Plato and Aristotle in Greek. He is supporting himself from his own
savings. He tears up letters from his draft board. He considers science "a demonic illusion of human *hubris*." He has already introduced himself to a noted classics scholar on the faculty, although
school has not begun. He has obviously wrestled with life's
profoundest questions, but he has made mediocre grades and will
continue to perform well below Orson at Harvard. He easily charms
a female student to whom Orson feels attracted. Although he does
not make the wrestling team, he easily and even gently overcomes
Orson when he jumps him during an argument over whether to
return the money from a broken parking meter to the state or to give
it to charity. Orson finds himself on the floor seeing Hub upside
down, just as his world is turning topsy-turvy because of Hub.

Just meeting Hub makes Orson frightened for the first time to be
at Harvard, and he becomes increasingly unsettled. He always
thinks the men on his hall are laughing at him. Hub is offensively
tidy, industrious, and considerate. By spring Orson can not sleep.
"His courses became four parallel puzzles." Voltaire's indictment of
God impresses him. The existence of other languages rattles him.
For no particular reason, he becomes convinced.that his hometown
girlfriend has been unfaithful to him (with Spotted Elk, no less). His
chest hurts when Hub tears up a letter from the draft board. In his
hatred of Hub, he becomes obsessed with him. His eczema gets
worse, and he is on his way to the mental-health office to head off a
nervous breakdown when another man on the hall relieves the pressure by having one before he gets to it.

The two men part after that first year, and although they both
graduate from Harvard, their lives go in the radically different directions that their freshman incompatibility might have presaged. Hub
finally gets conscientious-objector status, although he is prepared to
go to jail and has plans to complete a three-year reading list and
memorize the four Gospels in Greek during his incarceration. He
graduates from seminary and for a while combines an assistant rec-
torship with playing piano in a bar (in clerical collar) in Baltimore.
He works among the Bantus in South Africa until the government
asks him to leave. He then goes first to Nigeria and then to Madagas-
car, where, according to his last Christmas card to Orson, he is a
"combination missionary, political agitator, and soccer coach."

Orson finishes as the roommate of "two other colorless pre-med
students" for three years. He marries his hometown sweetheart,

completes the Yale School of Medicine, interns, and returns to his hometown, where he becomes the father of four children, remains as the only doctor in town after his father's death, wins perhaps more respect if not as much love as his father for his medical service and good works, and plays golf. "He is honorable and irritable." He is exactly the person he planned to be except for one thing. "He never prays." He also feels the old exasperation return when he receives Hub's Christmas card. Although it is unlike him, he mislays it and never answers it.

So threatened is Orson by the strangeness, the otherness, of Hub that he walls himself in as protection against further unsettling experiences. He does well. He helps people. He follows the script that he had drafted in his imagination. In the process, however, he closes himself against any invasion of his life by "the other," and he is content to view life through the lenses he had in place when he arrived at college because the roommate with the searching, fishy eyes has turned him upside down, not just in their scuffle but in their experience together. So turned off is he by Hub and his way of praying and living, that he closes that door rather than risk the unsettling effect of divine companionship. In Hub's seriousness about life, there is a playfulness that tries everything. In Orson's seriousness about himself, there is a cautiousness that risks nothing.

Another suggestion for putting ourselves in others' shoes is to strip ourselves *in theory* of any privileges we enjoy in actuality by an exercise of our rationality in order to imagine a just society for everyone. *A Theory of Justice*, by John Rawls, makes such a proposal. The person who might contract to live in a particular society is asked to go behind a "veil of ignorance." This veil screens out any knowledge of the position, privilege, or other assets that the person would have or not have in the society. Rawls believes that people would, from such a remove, want (1) to guarantee liberty for everyone so long as the exercise of it did not infringe on the liberty of others and (2) to assure that any inequalities of station in the society would be justifiable only on two conditions. The positions of greater privilege and power should be open to people who qualify for them. There would be no barriers of race, sex, or class to occupancy of these slots. The differences in income involved would be justified only if the differences benefit everyone; for instance, if higher pay for people in the professions meant the best people entered those professions and they made their services available to all people, their greater privilege might be socially acceptable. Behind the veil we should be especially protective of the least advantaged because we could very easily be among them.[29]

Rawls's exercise serves a useful purpose: it has pushed many thoughtful students of his work to reexamine their ethical and politi-

cal stances. However, its contractual approach to societal arrangements fails to find us where we are, namely already located in social
systems that most of us can choose to leave by the hardest effort and
only by electing to join some other actual societal group with its
already-existing arrangements, privileges, and inequalities. He asks
us to remove ourselves from the contexts we actually inhabit and
think as though we were not the people we actually are and will be
when the veil is taken down. He would have us believe that self-
interest will lead us to assure minimal conditions of well-being for
the least advantaged from behind the veil, but that it will not lead us
to cater to our own interests to the possible neglect of those of
others as we function in "the real world."

There is a subtle difference between the moral imperative to identify with the least advantaged in actual conditions of deprivation and
discrimination and the enlightened self-interest that imagines a society with enough entitlements to cushion a person's fall if hard times
come. One of the practical problems with the Rawlsian proposal is
that most Americans persist in the belief that they and their children
will not be found among the poor in any society they can imagine.
Rawls's "natural lottery," which forces us to play with the cards we
drew rather than the ones we think we deserve, is a crucial insight
that Americans are loath to incorporate into their stories.

On the current theological scene, various theologies of liberation
provide a potent push toward our putting ourselves in the others'
shoes. They bring into bold relief some aspects of that challenge that
the other proposals we have reviewed have treated indirectly, if at
all. They insist that people recognize the systemic and ideological
causes of some people's oppression of other people. Siding with the
oppressed means much more than learning to feel their hurts, hear
their cries, and work for a society that gives them more opportunity.
It means expressing solidarity with the oppressed by joining political
movements that push for changes in political systems and economic
systems that perpetuate injustice and oppression. To help people,
we have to change systems. The oppressors who profit from the
status quo need liberation as well as those who are exploited by it.

The conflict liberation theology presents as the prelude to justice
is often the necessary catalyst for getting the attention of those in
power and even for bringing people to a new perspective on long-
standing conditions of dehumanization. Yet, if our taking sides offers
us no way of moving beyond the "us" against "them" antagonisms
to affirmations of common humanity and reconciled community, our
liberation struggles can lead to new forms of oppression. In Jesus'
encounter with Zacchaeus, the rich tax collector who had been an
oppressor of Jesus' people, he recognized that Zacchaeus was also a
person who was oppressed and impoverished in his own way. (Luke

19:1–10.) Everyone in town would have been happy to tell him to "go climb a tree," whether he was interested in seeing over the crowd or not. By reaching out to him and going home with him, Jesus created a bond of love that enabled Zacchaeus to become an agent of redress and restoration.

Rosemary Ruether offers cogent insight about the "alienated oppressor," the person who enjoys a privileged position as an intellectual or a professional and who benefits from continuing to function within systems and institutions that help to perpetuate or even exacerbate injustice. To abandon one's place may be to forfeit a position from which one can work most effectively to bring about change. "The role of mediatorship in his own community" is probably "the only role in which he can be useful to them [the oppressed]," even though the oppressed may at times find that idea hard to accept. As Ruether states it,

> In other words, they do not need him primarily to join what they are doing, but to play a complementary role in relation to that struggle for self-determination, by helping to get his own community off their backs so they can have a place in which to breathe. In seeking primarily to join their struggle and move away from contact with his own people, he fails to play his vital mediating role which he alone can do for them and which they cannot do for themselves, short of successful violence.[30]

Thus, putting ourselves in others' shoes may involve returning to our own with a different outlook and agenda.

Despite our best efforts, we may find ourselves in the predicament of James Jarvis in Alan Paton's *Cry, the Beloved Country* when he finds himself unable to descend from his horse to stand on level ground with the weeping black pastor Stephen Kumalo. Kumalo is leaving to keep a vigil in the mountains on the day his son is being executed for the killing of Jarvis's son Arthur, the best white friend the black South Africans had in the story. When young Jarvis had surprised the black men who were robbing his home, young Absalom Kumalo had panicked and killed Arthur.

The novel traces the restoration of both fathers' sight. The black pastor discovers the fearful, impoverished, and degraded world that his son had inhabited in Johannesburg. Through the love he experiences from a pastor in a religious community caring for the blind, and from other blacks and whites who help him, he learns to understand, to forgive, and to sustain his son as he goes through his trial and faces execution. The senior Jarvis discovers his son's world, too, and he begins to sympathize with his son's view of the plight of black people in "the beloved country." As he sits on his horse, he is talking to Kumalo, the pastor who has long served in a village near his estate, but who has been a stranger to him until the tragedy brought them into each other's lives. Kumalo is thanking him for the agriculturalist he brought to the village, the milk he had sent, and the new church he was going to build because, as the black pastor says, "God put His hands on you." Jarvis assures Kumalo that he understands him completely as the black man below him gropes for words to explain why he is going to the mountain, and Kumalo is moved to tears. Paton writes, "And because he [Jarvis] spoke with compassion, the old man wept, and Jarvis sat embarrassed on his horse. Indeed he might have come down from it, but such a thing is not done lightly."[31] Yet he says, "I have seen a man [himself] who was in darkness till you found him." He saw things differently, and in a way he had left his own shoes, but he could not quite put his feet where Kumalo's were. Still, Kumalo understood that and accepted him.

Discovering Common Ground

Putting ourselves in the shoes of others any way we can and to whatever extent we are able is a way of behaving that enables us to see differently. "Behaving is seeing" is therefore as valid as "seeing is behaving." The goal, however, is not for us to become the people into whose shoes we have endeavored to step. To do that is neither possible nor desirable. For John Dunne, the person who "passes over" into another religious tradition also passes back to the one the person left. (And, in passing over to start with, we are conditioned by the story we have already lived.) As a result of the passing over and passing back, we reoccupy our own shoes as different people. We see our own traditions in a new way, but we become ourselves more, not less, in the process.

Hospitality to the stranger should lead to the sharing of differences and the continuation of dialogue, not to the vanishing of the host. We have something to offer to the strangers, just as they have something to offer to us. As Adele, one of the subjects in *Women's Ways of Knowing*, expresses it, "You let the inside out and the outside in." In what Belenky and the other authors call "constructed knowledge," the voices of self and others are integrated, though not equated. The kind of relationships involved are "inclusionary"; "we" and "they" are "intertwined and interdependent." In general, women are more comfortable with these relationships, whereas men lean toward "exclusionary" relationships that accentuate "autonomy and distance."[32] To become more intimate as partners or companions in knowing does not mean to become carbon copies or clones. To turn into the other person is to deny that unique combination of stories, relationships, qualities, and roles that each of us is. Listening to others in order to empower their speech does not mean that we must lose our voices in the process. It should mean that we have more to say when we speak.

If we engage in open dialogue and listen to one another's stories, we may find common ground so that we begin to act in light of a shared vision as well as from our disparate outlooks. In fact, unless we have some shared experience as members of the human race, dialogue will be impossible. We would be like strangers on a train who not only do not know one another's language or any third language in which to take refuge but who also consistently misinterpret one another's gestures and facial expressions. It would be dull if we had everything in common and nothing distinctive, but it is disastrous if our dialogue discovers no common ground on which we can stand.

Without some measure of mutual trust and mutual respect, there can be no dialogue, and the more genuine dialogue takes place, the more mutual trust and respect will develop. If either party is addressed as a hopeless case, the conversation will be short and the war may be long. Regarding conflicts between the oppressed and the oppressors, Rosemary Ruether observes, "Only when protest and response remain in dialogue in such a way that the society which is condemned is also addressed as a community which has fallen away from its own authentic promise, can there be liberation without ultimate violence; a liberation that can end in reconciliation and new brotherhood."[33]

The work of Cassell, Kleinman, Zaner, and others on dialogue between health-care providers and patients has implications for all relations between professionals and the people they supposedly serve. What is more, the context of trust and engagement in attentive listening without attempting to control each other sets a tone in any relationship that will make more good neighbors than good fences will. Fences may be necessary sometimes, but in a true "neighborhood" of any size and type, there must be well-worn paths through, around, and over them. As the authors of *Women's Ways of Knowing* assert, in groups in which people can criticize each other and still feel connected to each other in mutual trust and appreciation, "authority . . . rests not on power or status or certification but on commonality of experience."[34]

When we share each other's stories and stand in one another's shoes, we will discover some common ground.[35] Are there any particular stories we should be telling one another that would enhance the likelihood of such discovery and give moral substance to our commonality? Can shared stories give us shared images, metaphors, and myths with which to imagine a shared world? Yes, we can talk about our common planet and our common fate, even if we do not share a common faith.

   Talk about our common planet would involve us in contemplation of the consequences of an exchange of nuclear weapons for life on this planet. Whatever else we may not have in common, we do live under a common cloud. It would direct our eyes upward to depleted ozone layers and greenhouse effects and acid rain. It would direct our gaze outward to the disappearance of forests, the shrinkage of tillable land, the dying of parts of our oceans, and the victimization of animal life. It would direct our attention downward to buried hazardous wastes and fouled water supplies. It would direct our scrutiny inward to the effects of carcinogens, other toxic chemicals, and unhealthy diets on our own bodies and those of others. A common planet assures that we have a future in common even if we have not affirmed our commonality in the past. In the words of Gregg Easterbrook's special environmental report in *Newsweek*, "Cleaning Up Our Mess," "Perhaps the environment, the place where we all must live, will become the bond that finally brings the nations of the world together."[36]

   According to Easterbrook, world forest acreage has declined about 15 percent over the past century, and the rate is increasing rapidly, especially in South America. Of course the poor of South America need land and work, and we can hardly justify being judgmental when we both contribute to their deforestation problems and create our own. Millions of Peruvian forests disappear so that coca can be grown to cater to North American and European cocaine habits. Coca growers also dump millions of gallons of toxic wastes into Peru's streams. In Brazil, with the encouragement of governmental economic incentives, millions of acres of tropical forests perish to create large cattle ranches to produce cheap beef for fast food restaurants in the United States. Mexico and other Central American countries are similarly affected and afflicted. In our own Northwest, forests are being drastically depleted as companies attempt to avert takeovers or capitalize on the sale of timber after takeovers. Lumber companies and their workers are fighting for economic survival too. Around our metropolises, polluted air chokes us, green belts disappear, communities perish, and we all are impoverished in the process.

   The big picture shows the loss of eleven million acres a year and a potential rise in sea level due to global warming that could eliminate agriculture on many river deltas and flood plains and even inundate coastal areas.[37] Tom Wicker cites estimates that there will be no forests at all by the year 2017 in Nigeria, the Ivory Coast, Sri Lanka, Costa Rica, and El Salvador.[38] So the carbon dioxide concentration swells, and our planetary greenhouse warms.

   If we are looking for stories that our human race can hold in common, we may need to add some ecological martyrs to such martyrs for human liberation as Gandhi and King. When Brazilian rubber-tapper union leader Francisco Mendes Filho was shot and killed in December of 1988, evidently for opposing the deforestation process just described, and Peruvian environmental journalist Barbara D'Achille was captured and stoned by the Shining Path guerrillas because of her writing against the devastation wrought by coca production, they died for all of us. Their stories could bind very diverse people together.

Talk about our common fate would, of course, include the threats to our common planet, but it would also involve us in sober reflection on the accidents of birth and our common situation as what Herbert Spiegelberg has called "settlers or squatters" in "a universe we never made." As "fellows in the fate of existence," we all should know something about the unfairness of the accidents of birth. Our sex, color, place or lack of place, nation, generation, health or sickness, looks, physique, family, class, and religion are more conditions into which we have been put than they are characteristics we have chosen. The homeless may gain a homeland; people can change citizenship; we can do things that normally will maintain and even improve our health; we can forsake our family; we can abandon a religious tradition and entertain a new myth or worldview, and we can even have plastic surgery. Still, the conditions we are correcting have had an effect on us. Realizing the importance of the accidents of our condition is crucial for the appreciation of what Spiegelberg calls Albert Schweitzer's second moral principle, "his other thought," that is, "Good fortune obligates."[39] (His first thought was his better-known "reverence for life.")

What does good fortune obligate us to do? It obliges us to work to cancel the cruel inequalities of birth, to change the conditions that people endure because of fate rather than their own deserts. In fairness, we should acknowledge that what has happened to others could just as easily have happened to us, and that what has happened to us could have happened to them. Since we are "fellow victims," we are morally obligated to be "fellow agents" to do something about the inequalities of birth.[40] The difference between the fellows approach and Rawls's veil of ignorance is that fellow victims are looking at actual conditions they either know directly or could have inherited, and they are bound together in their actual fatedness instead of contracted in anticipation of the slings and arrows of a possible natural lottery.

The growing presence of chronic illness in an aging American population should serve as a telling example. If they have eyes to see it, givers of care and support have a fellowship with the victims in the frailty of our common human condition. The well and able-bodied should recognize that they occupy that condition only temporarily in what Bruce Jennings, Daniel Callahan, and Arthur Caplan call "a community of common humanness and vulnerability."[41] With this understanding, the young and the old, the well and the ill cannot be pitted against each other in an intergenerational conflict over access to assistance.

The third possibility for common ground is a fellowship based on faith. To move to such a bond is to move beyond the sharing and comparing of our personal experiences to the worldviews and myths we considered in the last chapter. Of course, sharing a common worldview or myth provides people with common ground on which to stand, but affirmations of faith can bond us to others even if they do not share our particular religious tradition. If we believe that all of humanity is the family of God and that all that exists is the creation of God, then we have something in common not only with other people but also with animal and plant life. For us that commonality exists whether everyone it includes believes as we do or not. If, as Hinduism believes, everything is part of one reality, all human and animal life is united. Not everyone recognizes that unity, but those who do will relate even to those who do not in light of that knowledge. If, as Christianity confesses, Jesus Christ died for everyone and therefore we are all already reconciled to each other in a sense, whether we act as though we are or not, there is common ground.

If people traverse any of these paths to common ground, they have moved beyond "us" against "them." They will have learned to tell better stories about themselves because they are no longer trapped within the confines of their own narrow experience and they have shed some of the blinders that block vision of a shared horizon. We are suggesting, then, that there are tests of stories just as there are tests of metaphors, myths, and institutions. We are also admitting, however, that we stand within some worldview or myth as we make our evaluation. Discovering a planetary community and a planetary story in which to "reason together" and make sense to one another is virtually impossible if our myths or worldviews will not entertain such thoughts.

Measuring the Stories

In French, *conscience* is the word for both conscience and consciousness. Perception and moral integrity are appropriately united as we have argued in these pages. If the word literally means "knowing with," both our perception and our sense of the rightness or wrongness of what we are and do is conditioned by the others whom we take into our consciences, whose visions we entertain, whose voices we hear, or into whose consciousness we enter. The inner dialogue of conscience is shaped most by the outer dialogues we value most. Conscience is not always a trustworthy guide, because the company we keep and the stories we are attempting to live may lead us astray. And, of course, we can lead our companions in conscience astray too. Trying on other stories and outlooks may remove one set of blinders only to introduce others. In fact, every set of experiences and every personal story carries its own bias, its own blinders, as well as its own lenses for seeing. Since there is no way to situate ourselves outside all stories or outside our own shared experiences in order to evaluate stories, what measures can we use for testing them?

The stories of our lives are potential visual aids, and not mere blinders, if we have the humility to suspect their adequacy as total contexts of interpretation and responsible action. Good stories admit their partiality and their need of insight from other stories. Good stories are ways of getting to know strangers, not walls for shutting them out. Good stories about ourselves not only tell where and what we have been; they hold out hope of where we might go and what we might become. Good life stories empower rather than imprison. Good stories talk about the integrity of the self no matter how diverse its public and private roles are. Good stories humanize others instead of stereotyping them and reach toward others rather than excluding them.

Good stories about our own lives root ultimately in those larger stories or myths that put us in our places and bring others into our good graces. Stories of our personal and group experiences must somehow answer to whatever worldview or myth sets us in an ultimate context of meaning, and these faith stories are in a sense answerable to the stories of our own experiences. Although we are adept at managing the news we receive that contradicts our reigning ideologies and worldviews, those views are "not long for this world" if they consistently fail to make sense of the stories of our lives.

Getting Our Stories Straight

We might say that our lives are ongoing processes of getting three sets of stories straight: the stories of our lives (our own experience), the stories of our culture (the myths and ideologies with which contemporary society surrounds us), and the stories of the roots of our faith (the traditions in which we ground our identities and affirm our fundamental loyalties). The point is not to make these three stories or sets of stories fall into line; it is rather to let the three keep challenging each other to deal adequately with the whole of experience (ours and others'), public and private, past, present, and future.

To squeeze everything into conformity with one's own personal story is to avoid the criticism and transformation all of us need lest we filter everything we see through the narrowness of one person's or group's limited perspective. To make everything conform to cultural myths is to ascribe ultimate authority to one society's or one era's way of ordering experience. Besides, our cultural myths often conflict with each other (for example, the "Triumphant Individual" and the "Benevolent Community"). To trim everything to fit a particular version of the Christian tradition or some other religious tradition is to deny the dynamism of any healthy religious tradition, to overlook the tensions and paradoxes in our own tradition, and to deify the vision of the particular people who first articulated our faith from the midst of their own culture's myths. We should also never forget that there are stories from other cultures, religions, and personal lives to enrich, expand, and correct ours.

Our aim should be to keep the three stories in dialogue and even in argument so that we do not become spiritually split personalities—attempting to insulate the various dimensions of our lives in airtight compartments. Dialogue requires some common experience and common sense from which to speak and some common language with which to speak. It does not require agreement, but it demands contact and continuing community. In fact we cannot continually keep them separate anyway, but we often avoid conscious assessment of their mutual interpenetrations. Religious traditions are shaped by every culture they enter and filtered through the dispositions and hang-ups of every adherent they gain.

Perhaps we never get our stories straight, but the dialogue goes on. We keep trying to find harmony and compatibility among our appropriations of our religious worldviews and myths, our selective assimilation and repudiation of our current culture's myths and ideologies, and our interpretations of our own personal story's meaning. In light of personal and cultural stories (my experience as a husband and the father of four daughters, and our culture's women's movement), I cannot accept the sexism I find in the Bible. In light of the biblical story, I cannot accept the widespread cultural ideology or myth that simplistically blames victims of poverty, homelessness, and disease. Because of what I have seen of such horrors as children's suffering from leukemia, malnutrition, abuse, and napalm, I shall never regard as God's will what people have botched, germs have caused, or nations have destroyed, no matter who claims that "the Bible tells me so." I shall insist, both on the basis of personal experience and on the basis of a particular reading of the Bible, that life is more gift than gain, no matter how often people justify their privilege by believing that they had it coming.

Summary

The interactive pilgrimage continues, and we have to keep trying to get the stories straight. Reducing them to one story would be a mistake, but ignoring their incompatibilities is injurious to emotional and spiritual health. Just as we lack integrity if we have a different identity in every institutional or organizational setting we inhabit, what conscience knows is hopelessly muddled if its mythic and storied contexts lack coherence. As often as we clarify the values and virtues that our various contexts exalt and expect, we unveil conflicts—within each institutional context we inhabit, within ourselves, among the people who influence us and claim our love, and among the institutions, images, and myths that shape us. This conflict and tension can be creative, but when the antagonisms among our contexts and within our consciences become too great, we either resort to separations and divorces among our various roles, myths, and images of the good life, or we find ways to assign priorities and to change our stories and ourselves to put our houses in order. If seeing is behaving, and behaving is seeing, we will be saved from optical illusions only by virtues of faith, hope, and love that are rooted in good stories and provide us with helpful audiovisual aids in the quest for common sense and common sight.

Notes

Chapter 1: Seeing Is Behaving

1. Horton Davies, *Worship and Theology in England: The Ecumenical Century, 1900–1965* (Princeton, N.J.: Princeton University Press, 1965), p. 128.

2. Stanley Hauerwas provides an excellent treatment of the priority of story over principle and also of the centrality of vision and character in ethical theory in *Vision and Virtue: Essays in Christian Ethical Reflection* (Notre Dame, Ind.: Fides Publishers, 1974), especially chs. 2, 3, 4. Hauerwas makes considerable use of the thought of Iris Murdoch in developing his position. Craig Dykstra, in *Vision and Character* (New York: Paulist Press, 1981), contrasts visional and juridical approaches to ethics effectively and emphasizes the importance of imagination, which roots in the emotions as much as the reason, for ethics. In their revised and expanded edition of *Bible and Ethics in the Christian Life* (Minneapolis: Augsburg Publishing House, 1989), Bruce Birch and Larry Rasmussen have added an illuminating section (pp. 58–62) on moral vision, explaining how it underlies or informs both our being and our doing as moral agents.

3. James R. Elkins, "Becoming a Lawyer: The Transformation of Self During Legal Education," *Soundings*, vol. 66, no. 4 (Winter 1983), pp. 450, 461.

4. Hauerwas, *Vision and Virtue*, p. 34.

5. H. Richard Niebuhr, in *The Responsible Self* (New York: Harper & Row, 1963), and James Gustafson, in *Can Ethics Be Christian?* (Chicago: University of Chicago Press, 1975), are exemplary explorers of the moral self's activity in interpreting what is happening. Hauerwas's *Vision and Virtue* illumines the importance of the story one is living for moral vision. More recently, Charles Kammer's *Ethics and Liberation* (Maryknoll, N.Y.: Orbis Books, 1988) presents ethics throughout as being concerned with what we should be as much as with what we should do. He gives worldviews and loyalties more prominence in the "moralscape" than norms, values, and modes of decision making.

6. Alice Walker, *The Color Purple* (New York: Washington Square Press, 1982), p. 176.

7. Joseph Fletcher, *Situation Ethics: The New Morality* (Philadelphia: Westminster Press, 1966).

8. James Gustafson, "Love Monism," in *Storm Over Ethics* (Philadelphia: United Church Press, 1967), p. 33.

9. James Gustafson, *Ethics from a Theocentric Perspective* (Chicago: University of Chicago Press, 1983), vol. 2, pp. 11–12.

10. Edmund D. Pellegrino and David C. Thomasma, *A Philosophical Basis of Medical Practice* (New York: Oxford University Press, 1981), ch. 11; Richard M. Zaner, *Ethics and the Clinical Encounter* (Englewood Cliffs, N.J.: Prentice-Hall, 1988), ch. 2.

11. Eric J. Cassell, *Talking with Patients* (Cambridge, Mass.: MIT Press, 1985), vol. 1, p. 6.

12. Waldo Beach, *Christian Ethics in the Protestant Tradition* (Atlanta: John Knox Press, 1988), pp. 43–52.

13. William F. May, *The Physician's Covenant* (Philadelphia: Westminster Press, 1983), p. 13.

14. Birch and Rasmussen, *Bible and Ethics in the Christian Life*, p. 62.

15. See H. Richard Niebuhr, *Christ and Culture* (New York: Harper & Brothers, 1951), ch. 1; Gustafson, *Can Ethics Be Christian?* chs. 2, 3; and Hauerwas, *Vision and Virtue* and *A Community of Character: Toward a Constructive Christian Social Ethic* (Notre Dame, Ind.: University of Notre Dame Press, 1981). Niebuhr regards faith, love, and so on as relational virtues, and Gustafson discusses insightfully "the sort of person one is." Contrary to Kammer's contention in *Ethics and Liberation,* I do not see that Hauerwas focuses moral concern on the self. Character and virtue as he envisions them are oriented toward other persons. As J. Philip Wogaman delineates in *Christian Moral Judgment* (Louisville, Ky.: Westminster/John Knox Press, 1989), "character" refers to a person's disposition to decide and act in certain ways. "Character is what makes us at least somewhat predictable to others" (p. 28). It is more than the sum of one's virtues, which are dispositions or tendencies toward goodness (however defined) in thought and action (loyalty, compassion, prudence, and so on).

16. Niebuhr, *The Responsible Self,* ch. 1.

17. Mary Field Belenky et al., *Women's Ways of Knowing: The Development of Self, Voice, and Mind* (New York: Basic Books, 1986), p. 18.

18. Flannery O'Connor, *Mystery and Manners* (New York: Farrar, Straus & Giroux, 1969), p. 144.

19. It was my close friend and Centre colleague Milton Scarborough who suggested, after reading a draft of this chapter, that behaving may precede seeing. It was my father who first brought it to my attention that Jesus has our hearts following our treasure rather than the reverse.

Chapter 2: Institutional Contexts: Cultures, Characters, and Professions

1. Wendell Berry, *Remembering: A Novel* (San Francisco: North Point Press, 1988), pp. 34–35.

2. Robert Bellah et al., *Habits of the Heart: Individualism and Commitment in American Life* (Berkeley, Calif.: University of California Press, 1985), pp. 71–75, 89.

3. Ibid., p. 335.

4. Erik Erikson, *Identity and the Life Cycle* (New York: International Universities Press, 1959); *Psychological Issues,* vol. 1; and *Childhood and Society,* 2nd ed. (New York: W. W. Norton and Co., 1963), ch. 7.

5. Philip Selznick, *Leadership in Administration: A Sociological Interpretation* (Evanston, Ill.: Row, Peterson & Co., 1957), pp. 39–40.

6. Bellah et al., *Habits of the Heart,* p. 334.

7. Robert Wright, "What Legacy?" Louisville *Courier-Journal,* Jan. 3, 1989.

8. Letty M. Russell, "Refusal to Be Radically Helped," *Reflection,* vol. 80, no. 1 (Nov. 1982), p. 8.

9. Reinhold Niebuhr, *Moral Man and Immoral Society: A Study in Ethics and Politics* (New York: Charles Scribner's Sons, [1932] 1960), pp. xii, xx, 47–48.

10. Christopher Stone, *Where the Law Ends: The Social Control of Corporate Behavior* (New York: Harper & Row, 1975), pp. 69–70.

11. Nathaniel Lande and Afton Slade, *Stages: Understanding How You Make Your Moral Decisions* (San Francisco: Harper & Row, 1979), p. 2.

12. LuAnn Krager, for example, sketches several implications of the moral principles of respecting autonomy, avoiding harm, benefiting others, being just, and being faithful for each of several roles of the administrator and of the educator in student services. The administrative roles she covers are those of planner, resource manager, organizer/coordinator, staff development facilitator, and evaluator. Her article "A New Model for Defining Ethical Behavior" appears in Harry J. Canon and Robert D. Brown, eds., *Applied Ethics in Student Services* (San Francisco: Jossey-Bass Publishers, 1985).

13. Peter B. Lenrow, "The Work of Helping Strangers," in Hiasaura Rubenstein and Mary Henry Bloch, eds., *Things That Matter: Influences on Helping Relationships* (New York: Macmillan Publishing Co., 1982), pp. 42–57.

14. William F. May, *The Physician's Covenant* (Philadelphia: Westminster Press, 1983), pp. 179–180.

15. The Business Roundtable, *Corporate Ethics: A Prime Business Asset* (New York: The Business Roundtable, 1988), p. 119.

16. Charles McCoy, *Management of Values* (Boston: Pitman Press, 1985), pp. 66–68. McCoy appropriates the work of C. West Churchman (*Challenge to Reason,* 1968) and Philip Selznick (*Leadership in Administration,* 1957) in his useful discussion of the corporation as character.

17. Edgar H. Schein, *Organizational Culture and Leadership* (San Francisco: Jossey-Bass Publishers, 1985), p. 6.

18. Douglas Sturm, "Assessing the Sun Company's Ethical Condition: Voices from Within," in Donald G. Jones, ed., *Doing Ethics in Business* (Cambridge, Mass.: Oelgeschlager, Gunn, & Hain, Publishers, 1982), pp. 102–107.

19. Schein, *Organizational Culture and Leadership,* p. 2.

20. John Ladd, "Morality and the Ideal of Rationality in Formal Organizations," *The Monist* 54 (Oct. 1970). This article is an oft-quoted source of the notion that a corporation is a machine that should not be attributed with any

form of moral agency. Peter French, Kenneth Goodpaster, and Charles Mc-
Coy are forceful advocates of the position I take. For examples, see Peter
French, "Corporate Moral Agency," in Tom L. Beauchamp and Norman E.
Bowie, eds., *Ethical Theory and Business* (Englewood Cliffs, N.J.: Prentice-
Hall, 1979), pp. 175–186, and Kenneth E. Goodpaster, "Morality and Or-
ganizations," in Thomas Donaldson and Patricia H. Werhane, eds., *Ethical
Issues in Business: A Philosophical Approach* (Englewood Cliffs, N.J.:
Prentice-Hall, 1979), pp. 114–122.

21. McCoy, *Management of Values,* pp. 41, 68.

22. Ibid., pp. 47–48.

23. The Business Roundtable, *Corporate Ethics,* p. 19.

24. William Muehl, *Why Preach? Why Listen?* (Philadelphia: Fortress
Press, 1986), pp. 68–69.

25. David Price, "Ethics and Legislative Life: Thoughts on Representa-
tion and Responsibility," *Working Paper Series on Legislative Ethics—Number 3* (Denver: LEGIS/50—The Center for Legislative Improvement,
1979); Richard F. Fenno, Jr., "U.S. House Members in Their Constituencies: An Exploration," *American Political Science Review,* vol. 71 (Sept.
1977), pp. 883–917.

26. Bellah et al., *Habits of the Heart,* pp. 119–120.

27. Ibid., p. 90.

28. James R. Elkins, "Becoming a Lawyer: The Transformation of Self
During Legal Education," *Soundings,* vol. 66, no. 4 (Winter 1983), pp.
450, 451.

29. James C. Foster, "Legal Education and the Production of Lawyers to
(Re)Produce Liberal Capitalism," *Legal Studies Forum,* vol. 9, no. 21985,
pp. 179–211.

30. Elkins, "Becoming a Lawyer," p. 461.

31. Wendell Berry, *The Unsettling of America: Culture and Agriculture*
(New York: Avon Books, 1977), p. 43.

32. Paulo Freire, *Pedagogy of the Oppressed* (New York: Herder &
Herder, 1970), ch. 2.

33. John Pekkanen, *M.D.—Doctors Talk about Themselves* (New York:
Delacorte Press, 1988), p. 15. (The article is a doctor's own recollection.)

34. Mary Field Belenky et al., *Women's Ways of Knowing: The Development of Self, Voice, and Mind* (New York: Basic Books, 1986), pp. 101, 113.

35. Parker Palmer, "Community, Conflict, and Ways of Knowing,"
Change, vol. 19 (Sept., Oct. 1987), p. 22.

Chapter 3: Institutional Contexts: Levels, Covenants, and Callings

1. The Business Roundtable, *Corporate Ethics: A Prime Business Asset*
(New York: The Business Roundtable, 1988), p. 10.

2. Christopher D. Stone, *Where the Law Ends* (New York: Harper & Row,
1975), chs. 15, 16.

3. Lawrence Kohlberg, *The Philosophy of Moral Development: Moral
Stages and the Idea of Justice* (San Francisco: Harper & Row, 1981), pp.
411ff, and Carol Gilligan, *In a Different Voice: Psychological Theory and
Women's Development* (Cambridge, Mass.: Harvard University Press, 1982).

After developing this position, I had the privilege of hearing Stuart McLean's paper at the 1988 annual meeting of the American Academy of Religion in Chicago, November 19–22. Entitled "Systematic Ethics—Some Rules for Ethics at Stages Four and Five of Developmental Theory," his paper appropriates developmental theory—particularly that of James Fowler—for ethics in a rich and effective way, using root metaphors at each stage. Although there is overlap between his position and mine, he deals with stages two and three in I-it and I-thou terms and not as organizational stages. He also mixes interpersonal and institutional understandings of covenant, whereas I try to stay with institutional forms, and he employs a contractual model at a different stage from its placement in my design. I find the thrust of his argument compatible with mine and stimulating for further reflection, but I have not modified my proposal as a result of his paper.

4. Stone, *Where the Law Ends*, ch. 18.

5. A. L. Schorr, *Explorations in Social Policy* (New York: Basic Books, 1969).

6. Charles McCoy, *Management of Values* (Boston: Pitman Press, 1985), p. 115.

7. See his essay, "Civil Religion in America," in Russell E. Richey and Donald G. Jones, eds., *American Civil Religion* (New York: Harper & Row, 1974) and Robert Bellah, *The Broken Covenant: American Civil Religion in a Time of Trial* (New York: Seabury Press, 1975). The original essay first appeared in *Daedalus* (Winter 1967).

8. Bellah, *The Broken Covenant*, p. 27.

9. William F. May, *The Physician's Covenant* (Philadelphia: Westminster Press, 1983), p. 175.

10. Max L. Stackhouse, *Public Theology and Political Economy* (Grand Rapids: Wm. B. Eerdmans Publishing Co., 1987), p. 127.

11. McCoy, *Management of Values*, p. 224.

12. Ibid., ch. 5.

13. Karen Strohm Kitchener, "Ethical Principles and Ethical Decisions in Student Affairs," in Harry J. Canon and Robert D. Brown, eds., *Applied Ethics in Student Services* (San Francisco: Jossey-Bass Publishers, 1985), pp. 19, 25.

14. LuAnn Krager, "A New Model for Defining Ethical Behavior," *Applied Ethics in Student Services*, pp. 45, 37.

15. Robert Pruger, "The Good Bureaucrat," in Hiasaura Rubenstein and Mary Henry Bloch, eds., *Things That Matter: Influences on Helping Professions* (New York: Macmillan Publishing Co., 1982), pp. 386, 392.

16. Stackhouse, *Public Theology and Political Economy*, pp. 25–26.

17. Michael Smith, "The Virtuous Organization," in Albert Flores, ed., *Professional Ideals* (Belmont, Calif.: Wadsworth Publishing Co., 1968), pp. 173–174.

18. H. Richard Niebuhr, *Radical Monotheism and Western Culture* (New York: Harper & Brothers, 1943 [1960]).

19. William F. May states in *The Physician's Covenant* that "a professional has an obligation to meet the needs of the *whole* public (its external catholicity), but also the *whole needs* of the public (its internal catholicity)" (p. 139). May's focus is the medical profession, but he makes the assertion

about professions in general. The position developed here echoes the covenantal standards he sets for both professions and the institutions in which
they work.

20. H. Richard Niebuhr, *The Responsible Self* (New York: Harper & Row,
1963), p. 87.

21. Robert Brown, "Creating an Ethical Community," *Applied Ethics in
Student Services*, p. 68.

22. Milton Snoeyenbos, Robert Almeder, and James Humber, eds., *Business Ethics* (Buffalo, N.Y.: Prometheus Brooks, 1983), p. 64.

23. Pruger, "The Good Bureaucrat," p. 352.

24. Craig R. Hickman and Michael A. Silva, *Creating Excellence: Managing Corporate Culture, Strategy, and Change in the New Age* (New York: New
American Library, 1984).

25. The Business Roundtable, *Corporate Ethics*, pp. 61, 78–104.

26. Smith, "The Virtuous Organization," p. 174.

27. The Business Roundtable, *Corporate Ethics*, pp. 65–76.

28. Ibid., p. 62.

29. Background for these comments about urinary incontinence was provided by Patricia Hess, a nurse practitioner and Ph.D., who teaches at the
University of California at San Francisco. I attended her staff training session at Vanderbilt Medical Center in the fall of 1988.

30. Mary Field Belenky et al., *Women's Ways of Knowing: The Development of Self, Voice, and Mind* (New York: Basic Books, 1986), p. 195.

31. Office of Technology Assessment, *Life-Sustaining Technologies and the
Elderly—Summary* (Washington, D.C.: Congress of the United States,
1987), p. 25.

32. Lisa Drew, "A Poor Rest Home Remedy," *Newsweek*, Feb. 6, 1987,
p. 56.

33. Edmund D. Pellegrino, "Professional Ethics: Moral Decline or Para-
digm Shift?" *Religion and Intellectual Life*, vol. 4, no. 3 (Spring 1987), p. 29.

34. Robert N. Bellah and William M. Sullivan, "The Professions and the
Common Good: Vocation/Profession/Career," *Religion and Intellectual Life*,
vol. 4, no. 3 (Spring 1987), p. 15. See also *Habits of the Heart*, pp. 66,
69–71, 119, 218, 287, 300.

35. Steven Murphy, "Resistance in the Professions," *Religion and Intellectual Life*, vol. 4, no. 3 (Spring 1987), p. 76.

36. Bellah and Sullivan, "The Professions and the Common Good," p. 19.

37. Douglas Sturm, "Assessing the Sun Company's Ethical Condition:
Voices from Within," in Donald G. Jones, ed., *Doing Ethics in Business*
(Cambridge, Mass.: Oelgeschlager, Gunn, and Hain, Publishers, 1982),
p. 108.

Chapter 4: Imaginative Contexts: Metaphors, Images, and Models

1. George Lakoff and Mark Johnson, *Metaphors We Live By* (Chicago:
University of Chicago Press, 1980). Ch. 1 treats the way in which we conceive arguments as war and otherwise use the metaphor to live by.

2. Bruce Jennings et al., "Ethical Challenges of Chronic Illness," *Hastings*

Center Report, special supplement, vol. 18, no. 1 (Feb., March 1988), pp. 9–10.

3. Thomas Vernor Smith, *The Ethics of Compromise and the Art of Containment* (Boston: Starr King Press, 1956), pp. 54, 74.

4. Karl E. Weick, *The Social Psychology of Organizing,* 2nd ed. (Reading, Mass.: Addison-Wesley, 1979), p. 50.

5. James C. Foster, "Antigones in the Bar: Women Lawyers as Reluctant Adversaries," *Legal Studies Forum,* vol. 10, no. 3 (1986), p. 288.

6. Ibid., pp. 296–297.

7. Michael Maccoby, *The Gamesman* (New York: Bantam Books, 1976).

8. Thomas J. Peters and Robert H. Waterman, Jr., *In Search of Excellence: Lessons from America's Best-Run Companies* (New York: Harper & Row, 1982), pp. 75, 101, 104, 164, 168, 169.

9. Bernard Malamud, *God's Grace* (New York: Avon Books, 1982), p. 80.

10. Sharon L. Parks, *The Critical Years: The Young Adult Search for a Faith to Live By* (San Francisco: Harper & Row, 1986), p. 116.

11. William F. May, *The Physician's Covenant* (Philadelphia: Westminster Press, 1983), p. 17.

12. Sallie McFague, *Models of God: Theology for an Ecological, Nuclear Age* (Philadelphia: Fortress Press, 1987), p. 34.

13. Ian G. Barbour, *Myths, Models, and Paradigms: A Comparative Study in Science and Religion* (New York: Harper & Row, 1974), pp. 6, 149, 155, 161.

14. Elisabeth Schüssler Fiorenza, "Feminist Theology as a Critical Theology of Liberation," in Gerald Anderson and Thomas Stransky, eds., *Mission Trends No. 4* (New York: Paulist Press, 1979), p. 204.

15. Barbour, *Myths, Models, and Paradigms,* p. 20.

16. Joseph Campbell, *The Power of Myth,* with Bill Moyers (New York: Doubleday & Co., 1988), pp. xvii, 31.

17. Daniel Maguire, *The Moral Choice* (New York: Winston Press, 1979), pp. 415–16.

18. Peter L. Berger and Thomas Luckmann, *The Social Construction of Reality: A Treatise in the Sociology of Knowledge* (Garden City, New York: Doubleday & Co., 1966).

19. See Barbour's treatment of shared experience, *Myths, Models, and Paradigms,* pp. 145, 177.

20. H. Richard Niebuhr, "The Idea of Covenant and American Democracy," *Church History,* vol. 23, no. 2 (June 1954), pp. 126–135.

21. Walter Brueggemann, "The Covenanted Family: A Zone for Humanness," *Journal of Current Social Issues,* vol. 14 (Winter 1977), p. 18.

22. Donald Schon, "Generative Metaphor: A Perspective on Problem-Setting in Social Policy," in Andrew Ortony, ed., *Metaphor and Thought* (New York: Cambridge University Press, 1979), pp. 255, 262–263.

23. Garrett Hardin, "Living on a Lifeboat," *Bioscience* (Oct. 1974), pp. 561–568.

24. Dennis Shoemaker, "How to 'Solve' the World's Hunger Problem," *Communique* (newspaper of the Synod of the Covenant, Presbyterian Church), vol. 5, no. 4 (Dec. 1978), p. 3.

25. Kenneth Boulding, "The Economics of the Coming Spaceship Earth,"

in Garrett De Bell, ed., *The Environmental Handbook* (New York: Ballantine Books, 1970), pp. 96–101.

26. Marshall McLuhan and Quentin Fiore, *The Medium Is the Massage* (New York: Bantam Books, 1967), p. 63.

27. Judith Wilson Ross, "Ethics and the Language of AIDS," in Eric T. Juengst and Barbara Koenig, eds., *The Meaning of AIDS:* Implications for Medical Science, Clinical Practice, and Public Health Policy (New York: Praeger Publishers, 1989). See also Susan Sontag, *AIDS and Its Metaphors* (New York: Farrar, Straus & Giroux, 1989). Plague, military (invasion), and plant (full-blown, and so on) metaphors are among those she criticizes. Any and all metaphors are suspect for her.

28. John Naisbitt, *Megatrends: Ten New Directions Transforming Our Lives* (New York: Warner Books, 1984), pp. 211–212.

29. Robert Reich, *Tales of a New America* (New York: Times Books, 1987), ch. 10.

30. Oliver Williams and John W. Houck, *Full Value: Cases in Christian Business Ethics* (San Francisco: Harper & Row, 1978).

31. CBS-Fox, "A Passion for Excellence," a videotape produced in 1985, listed in *National Video Clearinghouse*, 8th ed. The videotape features Thomas Peters discussing *A Passion for Excellence: The Leadership Difference* (New York: Warner Books, 1985), which he and Nancy Austin wrote.

32. Reich, *Tales of a New America*, ch. 10.

33. James R. Elkins, "Coping Strategies in Legal Education," in *The Law Teacher*, vol. 16, no. 3, 1982. Elkins discusses effectively the problems with compartmentalization, alienation, the compulsive worker, and the true believer as ways of coping.

34. Mary Field Belenky et al., *Women's Ways of Knowing: The Development of Self, Voice, and Mind* (New York: Basic Books, 1986), p. 227.

35. John David Maguire, *The Dance of the Pilgrim: A Christian Style of Life for Today* (New York: Association Press, 1967), discusses the aesthete, the victim, the aggressor, and the pilgrim. Carol Pearson, *The Hero Within: Six Archetypes We Live By* (San Francisco: Harper & Row, 1986), treats the innocent, the orphan, the wanderer, the warrior, the martyr, and the magician. See also David Harned, *Images for Self-Recognition: The Christian as Player, Sufferer, and Vandal* (New York: Seabury Press, 1977).

36. Much of the material on these two images appeared originally in a parents' day sermon of mine, "Self-Denial and Self-Actualization: Regeneration Gap?" which was published in *The National Institute for Campus Ministries Journal* vol. 5, no. 3 (Summer 1980), pp. 68–73.

37. Erich Fromm, *Psychoanalysis and Religion* (New Haven: Yale University Press, 1950), pp. 49–53.

38. Søren Kierkegaard, *The Sickness Unto Death* (Garden City, N.Y.: Doubleday & Co., 1954), Part First, 3 B. *Fear and Trembling* is included in the same volume.

39. William Golding, *Free Fall* (New York: Harcourt, Brace & World, 1955), pp. 144–145.

40. Thomas Ogletree, *Hospitality to the Stranger: Dimensions of Moral Understanding* (Philadelphia: Fortress Press, 1985), ch. 2. Ogletree uses Tillich and Sartre as examples of thinkers who virtually reduce the signifi-

cance of other people to our own drives for self-actualization. He discusses Levinas as a chief contributor to our understanding that the call of the other is the origin of moral experience, but he faults him for neglecting the need for the self to be centered and empowered before it can respond with care to the claim of the other.

41. McFague's chapter on "God as Friend" in *Models of God* is a rich discussion of the meaning and possibilities of friendship.

42. Sam Keen, *The Face of the Enemy: Reflections of the Hostile Imagination* (San Francisco: Harper & Row, 1986), p. 10.

43. "George Kennan Calls on U.S. to View Soviet More Soberly," *The New York Times*, Nov. 18, 1981.

44. Philip Keane, *Christian Ethics and Imagination: A Theological Inquiry.* (New York: Paulist Press, 1984), pp. 126–127.

45. Emily Erwin Culpepper, "The Politics of Metaphor: A Feminist Philosophy," a paper presented to the Philosophy of Religion Section of the Annual Meeting of the American Academy of Religion, Atlanta, Ga., Nov. 23, 1986, p. 11.

46. Wendell Berry, *The Unsettling of America: Culture and Agriculture* (New York: Avon Books, 1977), pp. 89–95.

47. Wendell Berry, *A Continuous Harmony: Essays Cultural and Agricultural* (New York: Harcourt Brace Jovanovich, 1972), pp. 159–164.

48. Wendell Berry, *The Memory of Old Jack* (New York: Harcourt Brace Jovanovich, 1974).

49. Wendell Berry, commencement address at Centre College, 1978.

50. Alfred North Whitehead, *Religion in the Making* (New York: World Publishing Co., 1926), pp. 16–17.

51. Nelle Morton, *The Journey Is Home* (Boston: Beacon Press, 1985).

52. Carter Heyward, "Nelle Morton: On Her Way," *Christianity and Crisis*, vol. 45, no. 17 (Oct. 28, 1985), p. 430.

53. Letty Russell, *Household of Freedom: Authority in Feminist Theology* (Philadelphia: Westminster Press, 1987), p. 57.

54. Robert M. Sade, "Medical Care as a Right: A Refutation," in Stanley Joel Reiser, Arthur J. Dyck, William J. Curran, eds., *Ethics in Medicine* (Cambridge, Mass.: MIT Press, 1977), pp. 573–575.

55. Dan E. Beauchamp is among the writers who contrast the public health model to the market model. See, for example, "Public Health as Social Justice," in Thomas A. Mappes and Jane Zembaty, eds., *Biomedical Ethics* (New York: McGraw-Hill Book Co., 1981).

56. George Engel, "The Need for a New Medical Model: A Challenge for Biomedicine," *Science*, vol. 196, no. 4286 (April 8, 1977), pp. 129–136.

Chapter 5: Imaginative Contexts: Stories, Myths, and Worldviews

1. Robert B. Reich, *Tales of a New America* (New York: Times Books, 1987), pp. 5, 6.

2. Ibid., p. 40.

3. Robert Bellah, *The Broken Covenant: American Civil Religion in a Time of Trial* (New York: Seabury Press, 1975), p. 3.

4. Roger L. Shinn, *Forced Options: Social Decisions for the 21st Century* (San Francisco: Harper & Row, 1982), pp. 230–231.

5. Phyllis Trible, "Depatriarchalizing Biblical Interpretation," *Journal of the American Academy of Religion,* vol. 41, no. 1 (March 1973), pp. 30–48.

6. Lynn White, Jr., "The Historical Roots of Our Ecologic Crisis," *Science,* vol. 155, no. 3767 (March 10, 1967), pp. 1203–1207.

7. Henry Steele Commager, "The Search for a Usable Past," *American Heritage,* vol. 16, no. 2 (Feb. 1965).

8. E. F. Schumacher, *Small Is Beautiful: Economics as if People Mattered* (New York: Harper & Row, 1973).

9. Dieter T. Hessel, "Eco-Justice in the Eighties," in Dieter T. Hessel, ed., *Energy Ethics: A Christian Response* (New York: Friendship Press, 1979), p. 4.

10. Richard Grossman, "Growth as Metaphor, Growth as Politics," *The Egg,* published by the Eco-Justice Project of the Center for Religion, Ethics, and Social Policy, Cornell University, vol. 5, no. 4 (Dec. 1985), p. 3.

11. Donella H. Meadows et. al., *The Limits to Growth* (New York: Universe Books, 1972).

12. Arthur M. Schlesinger, Jr., *The Imperial Presidency* (Boston: Houghton Mifflin Co., 1973), p. 299.

13. John Hellman, *American Myth and the Legacy of Vietnam* (New York: Columbia University Press, 1986).

14. Michael Novak, *"Story" in Politics* (New York: The Council on Religion and International Affairs, 1970), pp. 33–34.

15. Ira Chernus, *Dr. Strangegod: On the Symbolic Meaning of Nuclear Weapons* (Columbia, S.C.: University of South Carolina Press, 1986).

16. Ira Chernus, "Mythologies of Nuclear War," *The Journal of the American Academy of Religion,* vol. 50, no. 2 (June 1982), p. 262.

17. Ibid., pp. 270, 272.

18. G. Simon Harak, "One Nation, Under God: the Soteriology of SDI," *Journal of the American Academy of Religion,* vol. 55, no. 3 (Fall 1988), pp. 497–527.

19. Ibid., p. 512.

20. Reich, *Tales of a New America,* pp. 235, 255.

21. Ibid., p. 102.

22. Ibid., p. 246.

23. Ibid., p. 180. Reich cites as his source of information James T. Patterson, *America's Struggle Against Poverty, 1900–1980* (Cambridge, Mass.: Harvard University Press, 1981), p. 172.

24. Ibid., pp. 174–175.

25. Kurt Vonnegut, Jr., *Slaughterhouse-Five* (New York: Dell Publishing Co., 1968), p. 129.

26. Reich, *Tales of a New America,* p. 296.

27. Ibid., p. 251.

28. Ian G. Barbour, *Myths, Models, and Paradigms: A Comparative Study in Science and Religion* (New York: Harper & Row, 1974), pp. 105, 130, 172.

29. Reich, *Tales of a New America,* p. 252.

30. Robert Bellah et al., *Habits of the Heart: Individualism and Commit-*

ment in American Life (Berkeley, Calif.: University of California Press, 1985), pp. vii, 71–75.

31. Ibid., pp. 44–48.

32. Ibid., pp. 221, 235.

33. For a full and insightful treatment of the values essential to the life of an academic institution, see Richard L. Morrill's *Teaching Values in College: Facilitating Development of Ethical, Moral, and Values Awareness in Students* (San Francisco: Jossey-Bass Publishers, 1980).

34. Stephen Lukes, *Individualism* (New York: Harper & Row, 1973), pp. 45ff. Lukes, a socialist, makes a forceful argument for the benefits of individualism along with his diagnosis of its fallacies. For a more extended treatment of the roots of American individualism and my assessment of its adequacy and that of alternative ideologies, see my article, "American Individualism Reconsidered," *Review of Religious Research*, vol. 22, no. 4 (June 1981), pp. 362–376.

35. Michael Ignatieff, "Modern Dying," *The New Republic*, vol. 199, no. 26 (Dec. 26, 1988), p. 32. Copyright 1989, United Feature Syndicate, Inc.

36. James W. Fowler, "Stages in Faith: The Structural-Developmental Approach," in Thomas C. Hennessy, ed., *Values and Moral Development* (New York: Paulist Press, 1976), p. 175.

37. Bruce C. Birch and Larry L. Rasmussen, *Bible and Ethics in the Christian Life*, revised and expanded edition (Minneapolis: Augsburg Publishing House, 1989), p. 45.

38. Reinhold Niebuhr, *Children of Light and the Children of Darkness* (New York: Charles Scribner's Sons, 1944), p. xiii.

39. Shinn, *Forced Options*, p. 233.

40. Barbour, *Myths, Models, and Paradigms*, pp. 179–181.

41. James Gustafson, *Ethics from a Theocentric Perspective* (Chicago: University of Chicago Press, 1983), vol. 1, pp. 292–293.

42. Hendrik Hertzberg, "The Wound That Will Not Heal," Louisville *Courier-Journal*, June 25, 1989. Copyright 1989, United Feature Syndicate, Inc.

43. Joseph Campbell, *The Power of Myth*, with Bill Moyers (New York: Doubleday & Co., 1988), p. 21.

44. Ibid., pp. 22, 32.

Chapter 6: Life Stories as Contexts: Transmigration of Stories

1. Michael Ignatieff, "Modern Dying," *The New Republic*, vol. 199, no. 26 (Dec. 26, 1988), p. 31. Copyright 1989, United Feature Syndicate, Inc. Ignatieff attributes this view to Arthur Kleinman, in *The Illness Narratives: Suffering, Healing, and the Human Condition* (New York: Basic Books, 1988) and Howard Brody, in *Stories of Sickness* (New Haven, Conn.: Yale University Press, 1988).

2. All the quotations and background information about the Brookside Mine case are taken from Tony Dunbar, "U.M.W. vs. Duke Power: Picket Lines in 'Bloody Harlan,' " *Christianity and Crisis*, vol. 33, no. 24 (Jan. 21, 1974), pp. 290–295.

3. Mary Field Belenky et al., *Women's Ways of Knowing: The Development of Self, Voice, and Mind* (New York: Basic Books, 1986), p. 167.

4. Thomas Ogletree, *Hospitality to the Stranger: Dimensions of Moral Understanding* (Philadelphia: Fortress Press, 1985), p. 1.

5. Bruce Wright, *Black Robes, White Justice* (Secaucus, N.J.: Lyle Stuart, 1987). Carl Siciliano and Meg Hyre, "Racism, Silence, and the Subversion of Justice," *The Catholic Worker*, vol. 55, no. 8 (Dec. 1988), pp. 3–4.

6. Andre Brink, *A Dry White Season* (London: Flamingo, 1979), pp. 81–82.

7. Ibid., pp. 89, 99.

8. John S. Dunne, *The Way of All the Earth* (New York: Macmillan Publishing Co., 1982), p. ix.

9. Frederick Herzog, *Liberation Theology: Liberation in the Light of the Fourth Gospel* (New York: Seabury Press, 1972), p. 66.

10. Joseph Campbell, *The Power of Myth*, with Bill Moyers (New York: Doubleday & Co., 1988), p. 174.

11. Henry Hampton, "The Camera as a Double-Edged Sword," *The New York Times*, Jan. 15, 1989. Copyright © 1989 by The New York Times Company. Reprinted by permission.

12. Ibid., p. 29.

13. U. S. Catholic Bishops, *Economic Justice for All: Catholic Social Teaching and the U.S. Economy* (Washington, D.C.: Office of Publishing and Promotion Services, United States Catholic Conference, 1986).

14. Ogletree, *Hospitality to the Stranger*, p. 125, n. 51.

15. Martha Weinman Lear, *Heartsounds* (New York: Pocket Books, 1980).

16. Ignatieff, "Modern Dying," p. 32.

17. Ian G. Barbour, *Myths, Models, and Paradigms: A Comparative Study in Science and Religion* (New York: Harper & Row, 1974), p. 175.

18. Daniel Coleman, "The Roots of Empathy Are Traced to Infancy," *The New York Times*, March 28, 1989. Copyright © 1989 by The New York Times Company. Reprinted by permission.

19. Larry Churchill, *Rationing Health Care in America: Perceptions and Principles of Justice* (Notre Dame, Ind.: University of Notre Dame Press, 1987), p. 63–64.

20. Robert L. Selman, "A Developmental Approach to Interpersonal and Moral Awareness in Young Children: Some Educational Implications of Levels of Social Perspective-Taking," in Thomas C. Hennessy, ed., *Values and Moral Development* (New York: Paulist Press, 1976), pp. 142–167.

21. Ibid., p. 154.

22. Belenky et al., *Women's Ways of Knowing*, pp. 113, 115, 117, 118, 144, 187, 189.

23. Richard M. Zaner, *Ethics and the Clinical Encounter* (Englewood Cliffs, N.J.: Prentice-Hall, 1988), p. 318.

24. Nel Noddings, *Caring: A Feminine Approach to Ethics and Moral Education* (Berkeley, Calif.: University of California Press, 1984), p. 30.

25. Kurt Vonnegut, Jr., *Slaughterhouse-Five* (New York: Dell Publishing Co., 1968), p. 169.

26. Ogletree, *Hospitality to the Stranger*, p. 117.

27. Philip Keane, *Christian Ethics and Imagination: A Theological Inquiry* (New York: Paulist Press, 1984), pp. 81ff.

28. John Updike, *The Music School* (Greenwich, Conn.: Fawcett Publications, 1967).

29. John Rawls, *A Theory of Justice* (Cambridge, Mass.: Harvard University Press, Belknap Press, 1971).

30. Rosemary Ruether, *Liberation Theology: Human Hope Confronts Christian History and American Power* (New York: Paulist Press, 1972), p. 15.

31. Alan Paton, *Cry, the Beloved Country: A Story of Comfort in Desolation* (New York: Charles Scribner's Sons, 1948), p. 272.

32. Belenky et al., *Women's Ways of Knowing*, pp. 135, 45.

33. Ruether, *Liberation Theology*, p. 15.

34. Belenky et al., *Women's Ways of Knowing*, p. 118.

35. Ogletree, *Hospitality to the Stranger*, p. 120. Ogletree sees hospitality to the stranger as leading to the discovery of common ground, of ways in which the meaning-worlds of each may offer answers to questions of the other. What Hans-Georg Gadamer calls "the fusion of horizons" may not occur, but if it does, people can act together in a fitting way because they see themselves in a common world.

36. Gregg Easterbrook, "Cleaning Up Our Mess," *Newsweek*, July 24, 1989, p. 27.

37. From a resource paper titled "Keeping and Healing the Creation," prepared by the Eco-Justice Task Force and issued by the Committee on Social Witness Policy of the Presbyterian Church (U.S.A.), pp. 22–23.

38. Tom Wicker, "A Death in Brazil," Louisville *Courier-Journal*, Dec. 28, 1988.

39. Herbert Spiegelberg, *Stepping Stones Toward an Ethics for Fellow Existers: Essays 1944–1983* (Boston: Martinus Nijhoff Publishers, 1986), pp. 215, 218, 199, 219.

40. Ibid., pp. 104, 218.

41. Jennings et al., "Ethical Challenges of Chronic Illness," p. 15.

Index